GENESIS 1–11

GENESIS 1–11

A Narrative-Theological Commentary

James Chukwuma Okoye, CSSp

 CASCADE *Books* · Eugene, Oregon

GENESIS 1–11
A Narrative-Theological Commentary

Cascade Books
An Imprint of Wipf and Stock Publishers
199 W. 8th Ave., Suite 3
Eugene, OR 97401

www.wipfandstock.com

PAPERBACK ISBN: 978-1-5326-0991-6
HARDCOVER ISBN: 978-1-5326-0993-0
EBOOK ISBN: 978-1-5326-0992-3

Cataloguing-in-Publication data:

Names: Okoye, James Chukwuma

Title: Genesis 1–11 : a narrative-theological commentary / James Chukwuma Okoye.

Description: Eugene, OR: Cascade Books, 2018 | Includes bibliographical references and index.

Identifiers: ISBN 978-1-5326-0991-6 (paperback) | ISBN 978-1-5326-0993-0 (hardcover) | ISBN 978-1-5326-0992-3 (ebook)

Subjects: LCSH: Bible. Genesis, I–XI—Criticism, interpretation, etc. | Bible. Genesis, I–XI—Commentaries

Classification: BS1235.53 O36 2018 (print) | BS1235.53 (ebook)

Manufactured in the U.S.A.   JANUARY 3, 2018

The Scripture texts of Genesis 1–11 in this commentary, unless otherwise stated, are from the New American Bible Revised Edition © 2011 (USCCB).

Imprimi potest
Very Rev. Jeffrey Duaime, C.S.Sp.

To Spiritans everywhere:
May the Holy Spirit be your strength,
And the reward of your labors and mission!

Table of Contents

Preface

I have taught Genesis from the historical-critical point of view. I have also taught it from the perspective of ideological criticism. For the 2016 summer course at the Catholic Theological Union, Chicago, I decided to approach it as narrative theology. The class was enthusiastic, and many seemed to hear Genesis again for the first time. This commentary pursues the same method of joining critical analysis and theological inquiry with the hope of understanding better and even praying with the Old Testament.

This commentary fills a gap. Multiple commentaries on Genesis of differing levels and approaches there certainly are. Genesis is one of the most commented books of the Hebrew Bible. There are also many articles and even books on the narrative art and the meaning of sections of the book of Genesis, for example, Jan P. Fokkelman, *Narrative Art in Genesis: Specimens of Stylistic and Structural Analysis* (Assen, Amsterdam: Van Gorcum, 1975)—you will need some knowledge of Hebrew for this book. Narrative commentaries exist on Judges, Samuel, and Kings.[1] But English narrative commentaries on Genesis, and precisely on Genesis 1–11, are few, as far as I know. Robert Alter, *Genesis: Translation and Commentary* (1997) comes to mind, a commentary more literary than theological. A discourse analysis that does theology from a Christian perspective is Walter Brueggemann, *Genesis* (Interpretation, a Bible Commentary for Teaching and Preaching; Atlanta: John Knox, 1982).[2] Two narrative commentaries that however span the entire Pentateuch are: Thomas Mann, *The Book of the Torah: The Narrative Integrity of the Pentateuch* (Atlanta: John Knox, 1988; 2nd ed. Eugene OR: Cascade, 2013); John H. Sailhamer, *The Pentateuch as Narrative: A Biblical-Theological Commentary* (Grand Rapids: Zondervan, 1992).

1. E.g., Gunn, *Fate of Saul*; Garsiel, *First Book of Samuel*; Amit, *Book of Judges*; Fokkelman, *Narrative Art and Poetry in the Books of Samuel*.

2. Cotter, *Genesis*, is a narrative commentary, though with greater focus on technique and form.

My hope is that this commentary will spur narrative theological efforts on Genesis.

I am indebted to trailblazers on biblical narrative. Robert Alter, *The Art of Biblical Narrative* (New York, 1981), was among the first in recent times to open up biblical narratology; his book treats some sections of Genesis. Everett Fox, *The Five Books of Moses*, a new translation with introductions, commentary, and notes (New York: Schocken, 1983, 1995 [paperback]), adopts a "rhetorical approach," focusing on literary remarks, indicating themes and motifs, treating issues of character development.[3] Others are Robert Alter and Frank Kermode, eds., *The Literary Guide to the Bible* (Cambridge: Harvard University Press, 1987); Meir Sternberg, *The Poetics of Biblical Narrative: Ideological Literature and the Drama of Reading* (Indiana University Press, 1985), which has become a quasi-classic in the field. Jan P. Fokkelman, *Reading Biblical Narrative: An Introductory Guide* (Louisville: Westminster John Knox, 1999), is written for the non-specialist. Yairah Amit, *Reading Biblical Narratives: Literary Criticism and the Hebrew Bible* (Minneapolis: Fortress, 2001). Others are Shimeon Bar-Efrat, *Narrative Art in the Bible* (Sheffield: Almond, 1989); and David Gunn and Danna Fewell, *Narrative in the Hebrew Bible* (New York: Oxford University Press, 1993).

This commentary is also theological. It does not stop at the formal elements of language and style, but investigates what is being portrayed of the nature of God, the life of humans, the other beings on earth, and the interaction between these. Under "Tradition" I seek to show how elements of Jewish and Christian faith have grown from attentive reading of the text of Scripture in various contexts in history.

I have in mind the needs of students who long for a critical yet theological entrée to the Hebrew Bible without the bulky apparatus and the source analysis of the historical approach. Pastors and ministers who have to preach the word of God will find much help herein. The well-informed reader will find engagement with questions they bring to their reading. Although the apparatus has been kept to a minimum, fellow academics will find herein a dialogue partner.

---

3. *Five Books of Moses*, xxxii.

Abbreviations

ACCS	Ancient Christian Commentary on Scripture. Vol. 1, *Genesis 1–11*. Edited by Andrew Louth. Downers Grove, IL: InterVarsity, 2001.
ANET	*Ancient Near Eastern Texts Relating to the Old Testament*. 3rd ed. Edited by James B. Pritchard. Princeton: Princeton University Press, 1969.
Ant	Josephus. *Antiquities of the Jews. The Works of Josephus*, 27–542. Complete and unabridged. New updated ed. Translated by William Whiston. Hendrickson, 1987.
Catechism	*Catechism of the Catholic Church* (1994; 1998)
1 En	*1 Enoch (Ethiopian Enoch)*
Enuma Elish	Babylonian Creation Epic
GenR	*Midrash Rabbah: Genesis*. Edited by H. Freedman and Maurice Simon. London: Soncino, 1977.
IDB	*Interpreters' Dictionary of the Bible*. 4 vols. Edited by George Arthur Buttrick. Nashville: Abingdon, 1962. With *Supplementary Volume*. Edited by Keith Crim, 1976.
Int	*Interpretation*
JBL	*Journal of Biblical Literature*
JETS	*Journal of the Ecumenical Theological Society*
JSOT	*Journal for the Study of the Old Testament*
JSOTSup	*Journal for the Study of the Old Testament, Supplement*
JTSA	*Journal of Theology for Southern Africa*
Jub	*Jubilees*

LXX	Septuagint
Mishna	The first codification of Jewish law (around 200 CE). Cited with small m., for example, m. Sanh 6:6 = Mishna, Tractate on the Sanhedrin, chap 6, verse 6. English translation used is Danby.
NABRE	New American Bible Revised Edition (2011)
Neof	*Targum Neofiti 1: Genesis.* The Aramaic Bible. Translated with introduction and notes. By Martin Mcnamara. Liturgical, 1992.
NIV	New International Version
NJB	New Jerusalem Bible (1985)
NRSV	New Revised Standard Version
Onq	*Targum Onqelos to Genesis.* Aramaic Bible. Vol. 6. Translated with a critical introduction, apparatus, and notes. By Bernard Grossfeld. Liturgical, 1988.
Ps-Jon	*Targum Pseudo-Jonathan: Genesis.* The Aramaic Bible. Translated with introduction and notes by Michael Maher. Collegeville: Liturgical, 1992.
Pseudepigrapha	Charlesworth, James H. *Old Testament Pseudepigrapha.* Vol. 2. New York: Doubleday, 1985.
REB	Revised English Bible
Semeia	*Semeia Journal*
Talmud	The Babylonian Talmud (500–600 CE). Cited with small b., for example, b. Sanh 6a. = Babylonian Talmud, Tractate Sanhedrin, folio 6a (pages are marked as a or b).
Tarbiz	*Tarbiz* (Hebrew) *Journal*
TDNT	*Theological Dictionary of the New Testament.* 10 vols. Edited by Gerhard Kittel and Gerhard Friedrich. Translated by Geoffrey W. Bromiley. Grand Rapids: Eerdmans, 1964–76.
TDOT	*Theological Dictionary of the Old Testament.* 15 vols. Edited by G. Johannes Botterweck and Helmer Ringgren. Translated by Geoffrey W. Bromiley et al. Grand Rapids: Eerdmans, 1974–2015.
TNK	The Jewish Study Bible (1999)

CHAPTER 1

A Narrative Theology of the Book of Genesis

> And so people supported by faith, hope and charity, and retaining a firm grip on them, have no need of the Scriptures except for instructing others. And so there are many who live by these three even in the desert without books. This leads me to think that the text has already been fulfilled in them.
>
> —AUGUSTINE, *DE DOCTRINA CHRISTIANA*, I, 43[1]

A Narrative Approach

Methods chosen are usually relevant to goals sought; each commentator brings a certain perspective to the text. He or she approaches the text with certain presuppositions, questions, and concerns or is already convinced of the effectiveness of some method for the exegetical task at hand.

Most commentators on the book of Genesis use some form of the historical-critical approach—form criticism or tradition criticism, social science criticism, or some other. In the historical approach, meaning derives from the author and is generally sought in the author's intentions and historical context and time. Many of such commentators have recourse to the documentary hypothesis[2] or some recent adaptation or replacement of

---

1. *Teaching Christianity*, 125.

2. The documentary hypothesis is the theory of four *written* sources combined in the current Pentateuch as systematized in 1878 in the Graf-Wellhausen hypothesis. The four sources are the Yahwist (siglum J) assigned to 10th century BCE, the Elohist (siglum E) assigned to the late 9th century, Deuteronomy (siglum D), seventh century, and the Priestly Writer (siglum P), mid-sixth century. A redactor of the P tradition is supposed to have dovetailed these sources. This hypothesis is under attack; the dating of the sources,

it, for example, the Yahwist as postexilic, the entire material as divided into Priestly and non-Priestly, D-Komposition and P-Komposition. For current trends in this area, the advanced reader may consult *The Pentateuch*, edited by Thomas Dozeman, et al.

Some commentators apply reader-response approaches which privilege the reader. The reader consciously brings his or her convictions and points of view to bear; the meaning of the text is "meaning for me." Strands of this approach are ideological criticism, liberation and feminist criticism, postcolonial criticism, and so on.

An increasing number of commentators have recourse to literary approaches. These derive meaning from the structure of the text itself and how it intends to mean. They pay full attention to how it does things with words, both with the form (the *how*) and the content (the *what*). Strands of this approach are structuralism, rhetorical criticism, and narrative criticism.

Meaning Is Never Divorced from the Participation of the Reader

> Left to its own devices by the maker, the text goes in search of a competent reader . . . [What is essential is] that which the text itself provides, the world it evokes and the values it embodies, and then, the confrontation, the interplay, the friction and sometimes the clash between all this and the reader's world and values.[3]

Nor is text ever divorced from context. To begin with, the text of Genesis is in ancient Hebrew and this has built-in conventions and patterns of meaning.[4] The text itself has had a history and there may be textual riddles to be deciphered and apparent contradictions to be resolved. A synchronic reading thus cannot dispense with all historical or source-oriented inquiries. For this reason, I sometimes call upon the so-called Pentateuchal "sources," for example, in Genesis 1 (Priestly Theology) or the flood story (Yahwist and Priestly Theologies)—the diachronic in service of the synchronic. For the nonspecialist, some concepts used by narrative criticism may need brief explanation.

---

their nature and extent, are under negotiation, but no consensus has so far been reached.

3. Fokkelman, *Reading Biblical Narrative*, 23–24.

4. "Nobody is likely to regard the grammar and semantics of biblical Hebrew as irrelevant to a literary approach." Sternberg, *Poetics of Biblical Narrative*, 11.

The Narrator

The voice telling the story is called the narrator, to be distinguished from the writer of the story. The narrator is also to be distinguished from the characters of the story. Sometimes the narrator's voice merges with that of the characters, sometimes it diverges or stands in opposition to it. Sometimes indeterminacy may result from irony, the implied author undermining the narrator.[5] In any case, the narrator wants to bring the reader to his point of view (in the context of Genesis, the writer was most probably male). The narrator knows everything, even the future, and what is in the mind of God and not just of people, and so scholars apply the term "omniscient narrator." Such omniscience is, in the first place, to be understood in a literary, not a theological sense: "It is not necessary to consider such a statement 'historically reliable' and assume a prior phone call from the Holy Ghost to the writer."[6]

God as a Character

In narrative theory, "God" within the narrative is a character created by the narrator. As such, one may distinguish the character of God and the manner in which he functions in different parts of the Bible. Fokkelman writes:

> The God of the books of Samuel is not exactly the same as the God of Moses . . . and something else entirely than the God of Ecclesiastes. Add to this the fact that the God of a devout Jew or Christian will always be different and greater than the image that anyone has of God. So let us . . . not immediately lock the narrator of the Hebrew story inside our assumption that he, the maker of the character God, entertains the same values.[7]

Yet, the *biblical* narrator presents God as omniscient and omnipotent, always trustworthy. Jewish and Christian faith equates the God of the Bible with the Creator; Christian faith further presents him as the Father of our Lord Jesus Christ. The literary and theological points of view can be in some tension: "God" as character in the story versus the God of faith. For how this commentary navigates this conundrum, see "The Approach of This Commentary" below.

5. Gunn, "New Directions," 72.
6. Fokkelman, *Reading Biblical Narrative*, 56.
7. Ibid., 153.

Characters

The writer propels the story forward through characters who speak, act, and interact with one another—Cain and Abel, Lamech, Abraham . . . Characters are generally *round* (complex, with many traits, developing one way or the other through the narrative) or *flat* (represents a trait or an idea, behaves in a stereotypical manner). Berlin works with three categories: the *full-fledged character* (round character), the *type* (flat character), and *agent* (a mere functionary; in Aristotle, the performer of an action necessary to the plot). As example of the agent, she invokes Abishag, the beautiful girl who ministered to David in 1 Kings 1–2 but with whom the king did not have sexual relations.[8] In biblical narrative, characters usually show themselves through what they do and say; character profiles are rare. The characters of the biblical story are to be distinguished from the historical individual: "Abraham in Genesis is not a real person any more than a painting of an apple is a real fruit."[9]

Plot

The plot is the sequence of events that make up the story. In Genesis 1, the ordering is in a sequence of seven days. Sometimes, the narrator anticipates or foreshadows events, as in the oracle at Gen 25:23, "two nations are in your womb . . . and the older will serve the younger." The narrator may also connect with the past through a *flashback*. A common plot is to break up the story into *complication* and *change* leading to *denouement*; another is to break it up in scenes.

Point of View

The point of view is the perspective from which a story or part thereof is being told, whose vision or interest is being portrayed. The word "behold" (*hinneh*) draws attention to a character's perspective, what he or she is seeing. For example, Jacob had a dream and behold, a stairway (Gen 28:12; NABRE unfortunately omitted "behold"). It sometimes yields dividends to discern whether words spoken portray the narrator's perspective or that of the character.

8. Berlin, *Poetics and Interpretation*, 23, 27.
9. Ibid., 13.

Gaps and Ambiguities

Genesis 6:4 contains a couple of these: "the Nephilim appeared on earth in those days, as well as later, after the sons of God had intercourse with the daughters of human beings, who bore them sons." Who are the Nephilim (literally, "fallen ones")? Are they the product of the mixing of the sons of God and the daughters of human beings? The text does not clearly say so. If the flood cleared all humans except Noah and his sons, how could Nephilim appear "as well later," as in Num 13:33 ("there we saw the Nephilim")?

The other elements of a narrative the interested reader will find in one of the introductions to narrative cited in this commentary.

A Narrative Theology of Genesis

One third of the Hebrew Bible are stories. A criticism of narratology has been that the movement from it to theology has been conspicuous by its absence.[10] Hopefully, not so in this commentary, which is about what the stories say or imply concerning our relationship to God, other human beings, and the world in which we live.

But what is a theological reading? We illustrate the drama of theological interpretation first from the text of the New Testament, "sell what you have and give to the poor . . . then come follow me" (Matt 19:21).[11] But can one sell all one has and keep a family? Did Jesus intend the abolition of family life? He did not require Zacchaeus (Luke 19:8–9) to sell all he has, yet, he said that "it is easier for a camel to pass through the eye of a needle than for one who is rich to enter the kingdom of God" (Matt 19:24). Anthony of Egypt (251–356) took the words in their rigor. Hearing this text, he divested himself of his inherited wealth and withdrew to the desert. Desert monks thus imitated the ideal of the early Christian community. Francis of Assisi (1180–1226) heard the same text of Matthew and forsook his wealth to embrace Lady Poverty. Another solution was to take the words in their rigor, but apply them only to those called to the way of counsels. Ambrose of Milan (339–397) distinguished the precepts (for all Christians) and counsels (for the chosen few). Still another solution: the text's rigor is for all Christians. Anabaptist Hetterites (sixteenth century till today) insist that Christ meant communal ownership and that private property is not

10. Kelly, "Discuss and Evaluate," 1.
11. Kling, *Bible in History*, 13–43.

Christian. A fourth solution: the text preaches poverty of spirit. Clement of Alexandria (150–215) speaking of the salvation of the rich man maintains that "what matters is poverty of spirit, not poverty of possessions." Martin Luther interprets the text to mean, "you shall have no gods before me" (applies when riches become idols). A fifth solution is to regard riches as a blessing (Calvin)! For him, the injunction was relevant to this rich man alone. For Gospel of Wealth televangelists, God wills riches for Christians, for "whatever you ask in my name I will do" (John 14:13). What a diversity of theological readings of the same text!

Coming home to the Old Testament, a text like Genesis 34 illustrates how perplexing a theological reading can be. Dinah, Jacob's daughter from Leah, went out to see the women of the land. Shechem, son of Hamor the Hivite, saw her, seized her, and lay with her *by force*. But then, he was attracted to her, and *in love with her*, and wanted her for wife. Jacob heard that Shechem had *defiled* his daughter Dinah, yet said nothing; his sons were out in the field. When they returned from the field, they were indignant—Shechem had *committed an outrage* in Israel, a *thing not done*. Shechem proposed marriage and intermarriage between the two groups. Jacob's sons insisted on circumcision of all males. Shechem and Hamor convinced their people saying, among other things, "would not their livestock, their property, and all their animals then be ours?" The people agreed. On the third day, when the pain was greatest, Simeon and Levi, brothers of Dinah, slaughtered all the men, including Shechem and Hamor, and took Dinah from Shechem's house. The other sons of Jacob sacked the city and all in it, including women and children, *because their sister had been defiled*. To Jacob's complaint that they had made him repugnant to the inhabitants of the land, they retorted, "*Should our sister be treated like a prostitute?*" God meantime asked Jacob to move to Bethel. A great terror fell upon the surrounding towns, so that no one pursued the sons of Jacob. Is God siding with Jacob, saying nothing about the abuse of circumcision, breach of contract, and wholesale and disproportionate massacre of a people? And the narrator? Is he conflicted? He tells us that Shechem took Dinah by force and defiled her, yet was strongly attracted to her, in love, and spoke affectionately to her. Was Shechem's love sincere? Did he win her over? Was she detained in Shechem's house or was she there on her own volition? Jacob's sons slaughter a whole people who had agreed to circumcision in order to intermarry. The narrator tells us that Jacob's sons made this proposal "*with guile*, speaking as they did because he had *defiled their sister*, Dinah." Is the narrator condemning or excusing the subterfuge? Jacob obviously feared for the safety of his family, but was his inaction and the initiative taken by Simeon and Levi, Dinah's brothers, because she was daughter of the unloved Leah? Wenham comments that by giving the last word to the brothers the narrator prevents moral closure, leaving the reader to ponder what should be done in a situation of competing moral imperatives—which is more important now, pursuit of peace or the vindication of a sister?[12] In Gen 49:5–7, Jacob attempts some closure by dispossessing Simeon and Levi, but hardly. The reader may want to reread the story from Dinah's point of view or give his/her own title to the unit, thus encapsulating his/her theological reading. How does your interpretation throw light on relevant issues in Christian ministry today, like rape, family conflict, violence, ethnic strife, self-defense, proportional response, or the virtues God's people should live by? You may also consider how this story fits into the whole, perhaps by checking texts like Gen 35:22; 49:5–7; Exod 22:15–16; Deut 7:1–5; 22:28–29; 2 Sam 13:21 that relate to the topic of the story; this is called intertextuality. We will delve more deeply into this chapter in another volume. But our perplexity with this text shows that the biblical text does not always give clear guidance to conduct, that theological interpretation is a drama in which one ever seeks to ponder God's word in relation to concrete circumstances that can sometimes be messy and unclear.

Theological interpretation is thus not reading texts to extract doctrines or *the* Bible teaching as if the Bible consists of only clear-cut propositions of faith or only clearly articulated moral guidelines. I agree with Sternberg when he writes, "the whole idea of didacticism is alien, if not antipathetic, to the spirit of Israelite storytelling."[13] He gives examples: divine election and moral stature are not aligned, there is no automatic or at least intelligible system of rewards and punishments. The stories often are not written from a didactic and moralistic viewpoint. Sometimes they offer models, but generally they simply tell the story, "hold up a mirror before us to help us see ourselves and reflect on the way God is involved in our lives in their skewedness and ambiguity." "We discover such 'lessons' only by bringing priorities and criteria to the text and ignoring the dynamic of the stories' interest."[14] Besides, the text of the Bible is silent on many important areas

---

12. See Wenham, "Some Problematic Tales," in *Story as Torah*, 109–27, here 119.

13. Sternberg, *Poetics of Biblical Narrative*, 38.

14. Goldingay, *Israel's Gospel*, 286.

of life. The Bible also contains diverse views on many issues, making the quest for the current will of God not always as easy and straightforward as some might wish. Partly because of these reasons, scholars come at the theology of the Bible in diverse ways. I outline four positions I have found particularly relevant.

For R. W. L. Moberly, the Old Testament is the *story of a people*; it tells of this people's life with its God.[15] Theological interpretation reads the story with a view to articulating and practicing its enduring significance for human life under God. Moberly chooses to start from contemporary debates and appeals to the text of Scripture. His entry point is contemporary faith and spirituality, hence his is a *Christian* theology of the book of Genesis. The patriarchal narratives can be dubbed "the Old Testament of the Old Testament," in the sense that they retain a similar provisional relationship to the Mosaic revelation as the Mosaic revelation itself has to the revelation in Jesus Christ:

> The interpretive process primarily works from Jesus to the Old Testament and from Israel to Abraham; the normative traditions of Jesus and Israel provide the models by which God's earlier activity is to be understood.[16]

From Moberly we learn to bring our convictions and criteria to bear on the text and that what we find must have relevance for our life of faith today.

Walter Brueggemann, *Theology of the Old Testament: Testimony, Dispute, Advocacy*, sees the subject of a theology of the Bible as speech about God.[17] Even when God speaks, the text is still Israel's testimony that God has spoken. The heuristic question then is: how does ancient Israel in this text speak about God? In focusing on speech, Brueggemann brackets out all questions of historicity—not what happened, but what was said. The *what* of Israel's talk of God is linked to the *how* of that speech (rhetoric). So he seizes upon testimony. Testimony happens in a *court of law*, witnesses are called upon to give their version of what is true and on the basis of testimony alone the court must decide what is real, with no access to the "actual event" besides the testimony. Theologically stated, testimony becomes revelation, that is, "human testimony is taken as revelation that

---

15. Moberly, *Theology of the Book of Genesis*, 17.

16. Moberly, *Old Testament of the Old Testament*, 145–46.

17. I also consulted Ollenburger, *Old Testament Theology*, 305–21.

discloses the true reality of God."[18] Israel as a community has rendered a verdict that accepts this testimony as reliable. But within her and outside her, alternative construals of reality were always readily credible, and so attention to Old Testament Theology refuses any reductionism to a single or simple articulation; it offers a witness that is enormously open, inviting, and suggestive, rather than one that yields settlement, closure, or precision. The differing voices need not be reconciled with the core testimony and they destabilize the character of God, who is just a character in the story.[19] Brueggemann allows all voices in the text to speak, without shutting down any of them in a search of closure or certainty. He alerts us to the need to hold in tension all voices in the text as enshrining human experiences in the quest of meaning.

John Goldingay, in *Old Testament Theology*, vol. 1, *Israel's Gospel*, purports to examine how the narrative of Genesis expresses "the faith implied in the Old Testament or the faith that emerges from the Old Testament . . . but to reflect on it analytically, critically and constructively . . . keep[ing] closer to the Old Testament's own categories of thought." He writes:

> Yet I want to write on the Old Testament without looking at it through Christian lens or even New Testament lenses . . . a statement of what we might believe about God and us if we simply use the Old Testament or if we let it provide the lenses through which we look at Jesus.[20]

Christians generally present the relation of the Old and New Testaments as follows: "The New Testament lies hidden in the Old and the Old Testament is unveiled in the New."[21] In other words, they relate to each other as *promise and fulfillment*. However, the church also teaches that the books of the Old Testament "are divinely inspired and retain a permanent value, for the Old Covenant has never been revoked."[22] Jewish believers read the Hebrew Bible in relation to their own traditions in Targum, Mishnah,

---

18. Brueggemann, *Theology*, 121.

19. Paul House judges that "Brueggemann's method leaves readers with no finally trustworthy witness, jurist, jury or judge." House, "God's Design," 38.

20. Goldingay, *Israel's Gospel*, 20–21.

21. *Catechism of the Catholic Church*, 129; see also *Dei Verbum*, no. 16, in *Documents of Vatican II*.

22. *Catechism of the Catholic Church*, 121.

Midrash, and Talmud. Goldingay teaches us to let the Hebrew Bible and the New Testament mutually illumine each other.

Finally, Jon Douglas Levenson presents an interesting Jewish point of view in "Why Jews Are Not Interested in Biblical Theology." Jewish, like Christian, hermeneutics is not monolithic and not all Jewish exegetes agree with Levenson. He states: "To the Christian, biblical theology is concerned with Christological issues in a way that excludes the Jew and finds no parallel in Judaism."[23] Christians look for one great idea that pervades and unifies the Hebrew Bible; Jewish biblical theology, if there were one, would be piecemeal observations appended to the text and subordinate to its particularity.[24] Judaism holds Torah as prior and normative, the prophets only applied it: "It is hard to see how a biblical theology that did not respect the doctrine of the priority and normativity of the Pentateuch could be Jewish."[25] For the church, the sacred text is word (singular) demanding to be proclaimed. Judaism sees it as internally argumentative, a problem with many facets, each of which deserves attention, hence the midrash collections always have *dabar aḥer*, another interpretation; there is far higher tolerance for theological polydoxy. Point is, the personal stand of Jew or Christian includes postbiblical elements: "the message of the Hebrew Bible is a function of the tradition in which it is contextualized."[26]

The Approach of This Commentary

This commentary interprets the narratives of Genesis with a special eye on their theological and spiritual import. Some scholars wrest biblical meaning from the narrator's statements, evaluations, and silences, and from what can rightly be inferred from the manner in which he crafts the story. The biblical narrator accredits God with complete trustworthiness: "Both God and the narrator must be trustworthy and hence are the benchmark of trustworthiness for all other personae."[27] Sternberg asserts that "the Bible always tells the truth in that its narrator is absolutely and straightforwardly reliable . . . [he] invests his dramatizations with the authority of an omniscience equivalent to God's own . . . this omniscience itself ultimately goes

---

23. Levenson, "Why Jews Are Not Interested in Biblical Theology," 295.

24. Ibid., 298.

25. Ibid., 299.

26. Ibid., 300.

27. Amit, *Reading Biblical Narratives*, 95.

back to God."[28] However, the question remains whether there is just one narrator and whether his voice is but one of several. Gunn asks:

> When Samuel-Kings is read alongside Chronicles, where is the reliable narrator? Where for that matter is the reliable narrator of the four Gospels? Or, to put it another way: Who among the four narrators is reliable? What *did* Jesus say?[29]

Narration is sometimes in tension with narration. For example, biblical images of God are not unitary. Genesis 1:26 has God say, "Let us create human beings in our image, after *our likeness*"; in Gen 3:22, the Lord God says, "See! The man has become *like one of us . . .*" The evaluation of human likeness to God differs in the two: in one, likeness to God is willed and established by God himself, in the other, it appears as something God looks askance at.[30] The image of the national God of Israel (Deuteronomy) varies somewhat from that of the unique and universal God and Creator of the whole world (Second Isaiah). The biblical text contains millennia of human experiences of the Ineffable which it attempts to express in words; the diversity of times and contexts has led to a diversity of conceptualizations. Further, there is polemic in the Hebrew Bible and this not only against the cultural environment that enveloped Israel. The Hebrew Bible itself is polyphonic;[31] the editing allowed diverse voices across time and place to have their say, thus recording the people of God's diverse experiences of God and the world. In the search for meaning, Jewish and Christian readers are guided by the total witness of Scripture and their respective traditions.

In this commentary, the Hebrew Bible and the New Testament dialogue with each other.[32] The Christian meaning of a text is seen as a *parallel*, not a substitute, meaning; supersessionism is the wrong assertion that the Old Covenant was revoked by God and replaced with the Christian

---

28. Sternberg, *Poetics*, 51, 90.

29. Gunn, "New Directions," 71.

30. Scholars detect here the differing images of God in P (Gen 1) and J (Gen 2–3).

31. Amit, *Hidden Polemics*, xi: "This canon is by its nature polyphonic, and that the multiplicity of voices found therein is a function of the circumstances of its composition and shaping."

32. "On the one hand, the New Testament demands to be read in the light of the Old, but it also invites a 're-reading' of the Old in the light of Jesus Christ (cf. Luke 24:45)." Pontifical Biblical Commission, *Jewish People and Their Sacred Scriptures*, no. 19.

dispensation. On the contrary, "Its books are divinely inspired and retain a permanent value, for the Old Covenant has never been revoked."[33] As such,

> Christians can and ought to admit that the Jewish reading of the Bible is a possible one, in continuity with the Jewish Sacred Scriptures from the Second Temple period, a reading analogous to the Christian reading which developed in parallel fashion. Both readings are bound up with the vision of their respective faiths, of which the readings are the result and expression. Consequently, both are irreducible.[34]

Further:

> To compose the sacred books, God chose certain men who, all the while he employed them in this task, made full use of their own faculties and powers so that, though he acted in them and by them, it was as true authors that they consigned to writing whatever he wanted written, and no more.[35]

Vatican II decreed as follows on the truth of Scripture:

> Therefore, since everything asserted by the inspired authors or sacred writers must be held to be asserted by the Holy Spirit, it follows that the books of Scripture must be acknowledged as teaching solidly, faithfully and without error that truth which God wanted put into sacred writings for the sake of salvation.[36]

Belief in the inspiration and truth of Scripture makes some readers gloss over, or not take full account of, difficulties and inconsistencies in the text. On the contrary, the question of the inspiration and truth of Scripture is rightly posed only when the reader attends to the text as it is.

> When dealing with a topic like the inspiration of Scripture, it is better to begin with the text as it is and with facts that ground it in the human experience of the authors. We need also factor in the fact that the Bible contains variant forms of the text and some obscure passages that defy interpretation.[37]

---

33. *Catechism of the Catholic Church*, 121.

34. Pontifical Biblical Commission, *Jewish People and Their Sacred Scriptures*, no. 22.

35. *Catechism of the Catholic Church*, 106; *Dei Verbum*, no. 11.

36. *Dei Verbum*, no. 11.

37. Okoye, *Scripture in the Church*, 49.

Pope Benedict XVI encourages interpreters not to gloss over the "dark passages" of the Bible.

> Revelation is suited to the cultural and moral level of distant times and thus describes facts and customs, such as cheating and trickery, and acts of violence and massacre, without explicitly denouncing the immorality of such things. This can be explained by the historical context, yet it can cause the modern reader to be taken aback, especially if he or she fails to take account of the many "dark" deeds carried out down the centuries, and also in our own day.[38]

Recently, the Pontifical Biblical Commission, *The Inspiration and Truth of Sacred Scripture*, nos. 104–36, took up the challenge. It considered historical problems and ethical and social problems. Internal argumentation and dialogue concerning the practical will of God is a function of the inspired nature of Scripture. Far from shying away from textual corruptions or inconsistencies in the text or trying to forcefully harmonize them, I have let these stand, understanding each within its own context. The reader thus gains a better understanding of the realities of the text for a more nuanced view of Scripture as "word of God in words of humankind."

Analogy of the Early Jewish and Christian Hermeneutics of the Old Testament

The approach described above reflects the early Jewish and Christian hermeneutics of the Old Testament. As concerns the Bible, interpretation is the quest for *religious* meaning and authority for life. Till about mid-second century CE, "Scripture" for Synagogue and Church meant mostly the "Old Testament/Hebrew Scriptures." Judean Jews read it in Hebrew, Alexandrian Jews and the early church read it in an extended Greek text (the Greek translation called the Septuagint, with seven books more than the Hebrew text, also additions to parts of some books). Jewish and early Christian hermeneutics were similar. However, Christians differed in this that for them the real significance of the Old Testament was witness to Christ. Both traditions, however, sustained multiple currents of interpretation.

The Old Testament itself embodies various interpretative processes. For example, Deuteronomy adapts Exodus-Numbers to new conditions of

---

38. Benedict XVI, *Verbum Domini*, no. 42.

life; Chronicles reinterprets Kings. The Old Testament employed *typological* reading of Israel's history in which events to come were portrayed in the patterns of past events, for example, Deutero-Isaiah speaks of the "New Exodus" and Esther makes the salvation of the Jews sound like one of the great events of the past, especially the story of Joseph in Pharaoh's court.[39] Jewish exegetes sought to reconcile contradictions in the text of Scripture; the text was made to speak to changing situations and new beliefs (for example, the resurrection of the dead) were integrated as out-workings of particular texts. *Jubilees* (second century BCE) retells the biblical story in a manner targeted to deriving binding norms of behavior from narrative. Other works of biblical commentary, retelling, and expansion are the *Testament of the XII Patriarchs, 1 Enoch, Genesis Apocryphon*, the Targums, and works by the Qumran sectarians, who developed the method of *pesher*, reading Scripture as if it were a detailed prophecy of events of their own time and interpreting it in the light of these events. This is very similar to what happens in the Gospels, especially in Matthew, who several times says, "this happened in order to fulfill what was said in . . ." Even before the Common Era, Philo of Alexandria (20 BCE–40 CE) used *allegory* to assimilate the Bible and Greek thinking. The title "rabbi" appeared in the first century CE, and lent its name to what is called rabbinic Judaism. Josephus (37/38–100 CE) wrote a history of the Jews (*Antiquities of the Jews*) which he prefaced with an interpretive paraphrase of the biblical account. By the first century of the Common Era, the Pharisees had developed a body of interpretations called "*oral torah*" beside the "*written torah*," both seen as handed down from Moses. Greek influence had led to the seven rules (*middot*) of Hillel (turn of the Common Era), which were developed into thirteen rules by R. Ishmael (mid-second century). Tradition arose that "no one may infer by *gezerah shavah* on his own authority," hence one must base such on authoritative tradition. Jewish interpretation (*midrash*) focuses on conduct: the text is used to derive rules for conduct (*halakah*) while aspects of the text are freely developed for edification (*haggadah*). However, midrash is often atomistic, making inference from similar sounding words, often with little regard for the immediate context (compare Christian use of allegory especially of the Alexandrian type). All Scripture is seen as interrelated and Scripture is its own best interpreter. "Torah speaks in the language of humans," that is, words need be understood according to linguistic usage. Two broad hermeneutic processes were *peshat* (the literal sense) and *derash*

---

39. Cf. Kugel and Greer, *Early Biblical Interpretation*, 46–47.

(deeper and multiple senses). By 200 CE, traditional rabbinic interpretation developed into a system codified in the Mishnah.

The Targums are Aramaic translations of the Hebrew Bible. They were oral and concomitant renderings during the liturgy for a populace no longer comfortable with biblical Hebrew and whose vernacular had become Aramaic. They were eventually written down, some before the Christian era (as fragments of Leviticus and a Targum of Job at Qumran attest). Four Targums are extant on Genesis or parts of it. *Targum Onqelos* is the official Targum of Babylonian Jewry (originating early second century CE in Palestine, but standardized in Babylon in the third century). The Palestinian *Targum Neofiti* 1 (discovered in the Vatican Library in 1956) is so called because it came from a college for neophytes, converts from Judaism, in Rome in the sixteenth century. There is also the *Fragmentary Targum*, and *Targum Pseudo-Jonathan* (a Targum with a pre-70 CE strand, revised not before the third century, and with later additions some of which are post-Talmudic and even after the Muslim conquest, since it mentions the wife and daughter of Mohammed, Adisha and Fatima at Gen 21:21).[40] Jewish midrash on Genesis is compiled in *The Midrash Rabbah: Genesis*, edited by H. Freedman and Maurice Simon. Rashi's commentary is available in *Pentateuch with Targum Onkelos, Haphtaroth and Rashi's Commentary: Genesis*. Easily accessible is James L. Kugel, *The Bible as It Was*, which compiles and comments on some of the Jewish midrash.

The earliest Christian interpretation of Scripture was theological exegesis—the sacred text as basis for preaching the gospel, pastoral care, theology, spirituality, and for disputes with Jews and heretics. Christians used the Old Testament to preach Christ and the Christian faith; the emerging New Testament treated the Old Testament as a prophecy fulfilled in the event of Jesus Christ. Paul regarded the law spiritually as a tutor (*paidagōgos*) unto Christ: "the law was our disciplinarian for Christ, that we might be justified by faith" (Gal 3:24). He rejected the force of much of its legislation for his Gentile converts. New Testament texts found details of the life of Jesus in the Old Testament, for example, the birth in Bethlehem. It sometimes wove the wording of the Old Testament into the story of Jesus, for example, Mark 15:24 (they divided his clothes) which John 19:24 shows to be a quotation of Ps 22:18. Christians used *typology* to match persons and events in the two Testaments. For example, the crossing of the Red Sea became a type of

---

40. Okoye, "Examination of the Non-Literal Exegesis in Genesis 1–11," 41–45.

Christ's victory and also of Christian Baptism.[41] The Letter to the Hebrews sees the Old Testament as a shadow of the New. Marcion (ca. 100–160) rejected the entire Old Testament; in the New Testament, he selected only ten letters of Paul and a sanitized Luke. For Gnostics, the creator and god of the Old Testament was the demiurge, a lower god, who differed from the God of Jesus Christ. Gnostics added their secret works to the Bible and employed allegory as the method of interpretation. The Gnostics invented the commentary genre. The earliest Christian commentary was the Valentinian Heracleon's *Commentary on John's Gospel*, fragments of which are preserved in Origen's *Commentary on John*. The dual crisis of Marcion and the Gnostics led to defining the canon of the New Testament. It also led to greater attention to context, insistence on the unity of Old and New Testaments, and a brief flight from allegory to the literal sense.

Justin Martyr (100–165 CE), *Dialogue with Trypho*, treated every part of the Old Testament as prophecy of Christ. Wherever God appeared in human form in the Old Testament, it was the Logos/Word Incarnate who appeared. Irenaeus of Lyons (ca. 125–202 CE) was the first to use the expression "*New Testament*" (*Against Heresies* 4.9.1). Origen (ca. 185–254) established Christian biblical hermeneutics as a real science (cf. *De Princ* IV 1–3). In *Contra Celsum* VI 77, he compared the letter of the sacred text to the human body assumed by Christ, the envelope which encloses the divine Logos. The literal meaning is for him not the ultimate goal of Scripture, but only an educative starting point (*De Princ.* I, Praef 3). That Scripture has a deeper spiritual sense over and above the literal sense is for him an article of faith: all Scripture has a spiritual sense, but not all Scripture has a literal sense.[42] He consistently worked with three senses of Scripture: the *literal*, the *moral*, and the *spiritual-mystical*.[43] Origen, nevertheless, paid great attention to the literal sense, for example, for the *Song of Songs*, he first worked through the literal sense before the spiritual sense. He developed the *Hexapla*, in which he tried to establish the correct text of Scripture. To

41. Across the Red Sea Israel gained deliverance and was free from the shackles of slavery; across the waters of baptism the neophyte gained salvation and the freedom of the children of God.

42. He gave the example of the Lord God planting a garden in Eden (*De Princ* IV 3:5).

43. Origen's three senses of Scripture stood till John Cassian (360–432) writing for his monks distinguished historical from spiritual understanding (allegory), dividing allegory into three: *tropologia* (moral), *allegoria* (typology), and *anagoge* (from earthly to heavenly)—"as far as we know, this is the first instance of a fourfold distinction of the sense of Scripture, rather than three." Simonetti, *Biblical Interpretation*, 119.

counter the excessive allegorization of the Gnostics, he insisted that spiritual interpretation be connected with the literal sense and confirmed by other Scripture passages (*De Princ.* IV 2:9; IV 3:4, 5). In the late third and early fourth centuries, two schools of Christian interpretation vied with each other: the allegorizing Alexandrian School, the icon of which was Origen, and the literalizing Antiochene School (of which the icon was Theodore, bishop of Mopsuestia, 350–428). Jerome (from 390–406) prepared a fresh translation of the Old Testament directly from the Hebrew, the Vulgate (*vulgata* = commonly used). At first a disciple of Origen, he increasingly insisted on the literal sense. When the Arians enlisted the plain and grammatical meaning of the text in their argument against Catholics, the wider church was led to rediscover analogy (language about God is symbolic). It developed the criterion of the *"rule of faith"* (first in Irenaeus). Augustine (354–430), a Latin rhetorician with no knowledge of Hebrew and who read Greek with difficulty, insisted that exegesis has only one task, to promote love (God and neighbor) and lead to the enjoyment of God. As criteria for reducing ambiguity and discerning possible multiple senses, he used the analogy of Scripture, the analogy of faith, and the goal of love. Like Jerome, Augustine began interpretation as an Origenist, but later tempered the use of allegory for greater use of the literal sense.

The Fathers memorized large portions of Scripture[44] and compared text with text on the premise that Scripture is best explained from Scripture. They read Scripture within the church and their interpretations were mostly in the context of liturgy and catechesis and aimed at the formation of faith and proper Christian living. They saw the divine intention of Scripture as connected with the mystery of Christ and from it they developed what became Christian dogma. The patristic use of the term allegory was not consistent. The Greek Fathers generally used two terms: *historia* (the literal sense) and *theoria* (deeper sense, allegory). But allegory can also be a division of *theoria* (as in note 43 above). Besides, allegory and typology are not synonyms. Typology is defined as "a prefiguration in a different stage of redemptive history that indicates the outline or essential features of the future reality and that loses its own significance when that reality appears."[45] The correspondence is seen to be historical, theological, in essential features (not accidentals), and divinely ordained. Allegory is correspondence

---

44. To be noted is that their text was the Greek Old Testament (Septuagint, abbreviated LXX, the Latin siglum for seventy).

45. Goppelt, *Typos*, 177.

between similar words understood as inspired symbols but removed from a historical context.[46]

An accessible volume on patristic exegesis of East and West is *Ancient Christian Commentary on Scripture: Genesis 1–11*, edited by Andrew Louth; and *Genesis 12–50*, edited by Mark Sheridan. The reader may also access a wealth of patristic texts on the Christian Classics Ethereal Library website (www.ccel.org). The succinct summaries of exegesis and dogma in the *Catechism of the Catholic Church* (1994) prove helpful.

Translation Matters

Narrative criticism operates best on the original Hebrew text. Translation hampers narrative art in that it renders invisible much of the language games in the original through which the text produces some of its rhetorical effect. I will draw attention here and there to important language games, but in transliteration.

Translators often face the dilemma of choice between fields of meaning. They determine what is the global message of a section of the text and align their translations to this point of view. Look carefully at these translations of Gen 1:2.

- And a wind from God sweeping over the water, TNK
- While a wind from God swept over the face of the waters, NRSV
- And a mighty wind sweeping over the waters, NABRE
- With a divine wind sweeping over the waters, NJB
- And the spirit of God hovered over the surface of the water, REB
- And the Spirit of God was hovering over the waters, NIV

The original is *ruaḥ ʾelohīm*; *ruaḥ* can mean wind, breath, spirit. *ʾElohīm* means God, or the plural, gods, but can be used to refer to the height or grandeur of something (hence "mighty" wind, NABRE; "divine" wind, NJB makes out the wind as animate divine element). While "spirit of God" (REB) is ambiguous, "Spirit of God" (NIV) definitely Christianizes the text and understands it as expressing an action of the Holy Spirit. The root of the verb *meraḥephet* occurs again only in Deut 32:11 where it refers to an eagle hovering over its nest (hence REB and NIV). The other

46. Cf. VanMaaren, "Adam-Christ Typology," 277.

translations borrowed the analogy of Gen 8:1 where "God made a wind sweep [ya⊠abar ruaḥ—caused the wind to cross] over the earth, and the waters [of the flood] began to subside."

Now and then I refer to the original Hebrew to illuminate the possible moral fiber of a text. For it happens that a choice among apparent synonyms can slant the meaning.

Finally, a look at the early versions sometimes alerts to issues in the text. Take Gen 6:6: "the Lord regretted making human beings on the earth, and his heart was grieved." Did he not foresee what would happen? Is he fickle? Can God change? Greek philosophy holds God immutable. The Greek translation (Septuagint) dissimulates the problem: "then God considered [enethumēthē] that he had made humankind on the earth, and he thought over it [dienoēthē]."

Transliteration Matters

I dispense with Hebrew letters and use only transliteration when it is necessary to draw attention to features of the biblical text. The Bible text used is generally NABRE (New American Bible, Revised Edition, 2011); the text of Genesis 1–11 being commented upon is given in italics. Other versions are indicated when used. Occasionally I use my own translation.

Recurring Themes Propel the Story of Genesis

The story of Genesis is divided into four cycles: Primeval History, Genesis 1–11; Abraham Cycle, Genesis 12:1—25:18; the Jacob Cycle, Gen 25:19—36:43; and the Joseph Novella, Genesis 37–50.

Certain recurring themes propel the story. In the first place, genealogies. Eleven toledot phrases, "these are the descendants of" (5:1; 10:1; 11:10; 25:12; 36:1, 9), "this is the story of" (2:4; 6:9; 11:27; 25:29; 37:2) bind the text into a unity. The human race multiplies in segments from Adam till all families are wiped out in the flood except for Noah and his family. Noah is a new beginning. From Noah and his three sons, Shem, Ham, and Japheth, the earth is populated, seventy nations and peoples, God having scattered them after the incidence of the City and Tower, Genesis 11. The genealogy picks up the line of Shem and traces it through Terah to Abram who becomes a sort of new beginning of the works of God. Abraham fathered

Ishmael and Isaac; the younger Isaac is chosen. Isaac fathered Esau and Jacob; again the younger Jacob is chosen and his children become the Twelve Tribes of Israel.

Another unitive feature is the promises to the patriarchs—of blessing, descendants/great nation, land, political supremacy. Then there is the offer of covenant relationship. And all through, Israel is reflecting on her election, what it means to be blessed by God, and what relationship this dictates in relation to the nations and peoples of the earth. In short, the destiny of Israel vis-à-vis God and the rest of God's creation.

CHAPTER 2

Genesis 1:1—2:4a

The Creation of the Universe

The heavens declare the glory of God; the firmament proclaims the works of his hands.

—Psalm 19:2

Introduction

Genesis 1:1—2:4a is a proclamation of faith, and is best read as such. The writer has reshaped traditions of the origin of the universe common to peoples of the ancient Near East to portray "the absolute subordination of all creation to the supreme Creator who thus can make use of the forces of nature to fulfill his mighty deeds in history."[1] The "creator of Israel, your King" (Isa 43:15) is also "God from of old, creator of the ends of the earth" (Isa 40:28). This means that "God's action which Israel has experienced in its history is extended to the whole of history and to the whole world."[2]

Myths of origin ground what is most essential to human life and society in the divine dispensation at the beginning of time. They justify societal institutions by relating them to the primeval structure of things,[3] for example, kingship as primeval gift handed down from the gods. The imperfections and painful situations of this life cannot compare with the blueprint "at that time" when things emerged in their perfect state. A fu-

1. Sarna, *Understanding Genesis*, 9.
2. Westermann, *Genesis 1–11*, 65.
3. I shall draw from my treatment of Gen 1 in Okoye, *Israel and the Nations*, 24–34.

ture will come when things will revert to their ideal origins—*Urzeit gleich Endzeit* (like beginning, like consummation). The writer exercised great polemic art, pitting the faith of Israel against the beliefs of neighbors.

The narrative is tightly structured, framed by an *inclusio*, and marked by a distinct style. The frame repeats "*God created*" / *bara* (1:1: *God created the heavens and the earth*; and 2:4a: *which God created in making*). A seven-day structure organizes the narrative. The point of view is from heaven to earth, hence the earth is focus of concern. A twofold process plots movement from heaven to the waters and to earth. The diptych is such that day 1 corresponds to day 4, day 2 to day 5, and day 3 to day 6: God first prepares the elements, then makes and installs the beneficiary. On day 7, God "rests." A seven-day structure of creation is unique to the biblical text and is found nowhere else. In climaxing with the rest/enthronement of God while alluding to the Sabbath, the writer makes the story of origins serve the universal reign of God.

Seven-day creation scheme

Day 1	light	Day 4	the luminaries
Day 2	waters separated Sea and sky appear	Day 5	fish/sea creatures and birds
Day 3	dry land, vegetation	Day 6	animals and humankind
Day 7	the rest of God—world as temple		

The style is solemn and repeats the command-execution pattern characteristic of the Priestly writer.[4]

- Introduction — and God said
- Command (in jussive) — let it be, let them be gathered
- Completion — and so it was
- Judgment — and God saw that it was good (very good, v. 31)
- Time sequence — and it was evening and it was morning

Obedience to the word of God creates harmony; everything is at its best when it follows the divine command. The word of God causes things to be, just as the prophets will show that the word of God also controls

4. Cf. Westermann, *Genesis 1–11*, 84.

history. The intended response is one of wonder, worship, and praise, as for example in Psalm 8.

PSALM 8

O LORD, our Lord, how awesome is your name through all the earth! I will sing of your majesty above the heavens with the mouth of babes and infants . . . When I see your heavens, the work of your fingers, the moon and the stars that you set in place—what is man that you are mindful of him, and the son of man that you care for him? Yet you have made him little less than a god, crowned him with glory and honor. You have given him rule over the works of your hands, put all things at his feet . . . O LORD, our Lord, how awesome is your name through all the earth!

The Text

In the beginning, when God created the heavens and the earth.[5] *Elohim* (God, god, or gods) is the common divine name that Israel shared with her neighbors; the verb here is singular. Israel's God stands alone, never was born nor became, in marked contrast with the gods of the cultures around. For Jewish faith, confession of the one God is the very root of faith; a heretic is *kopher ba-⊠iqar*, one who denies the very principle of faith. Genesis 2–3 will speak of *YHWH Elohim*, the Lord God. YHWH, translated "LORD," is Israel's confessional name for her God. The "God" of Genesis 1 is thereby identified with the Lord of Israel's faith, the one revealed in acts in her history. The history of God has begun. The God who brings order out of cosmic chaos can be trusted to bring order out of the chaos of Israel's exile.

When God created. The verb *bara'* always has God as subject. It recurs at the creation of the sea creatures (Gen 1:21) and of human beings (Gen 1:27) while rounding off the unit at 2:4a. Rashi[6] reads, *bereshit* as "at the

5. The Septuagint, followed by some versions, like NRSV, translated, "in the beginning, God created the heavens and the earth," suggesting creation from nothing, but this became explicit only later in the Christian Old Testament, 2 Macc 7:28, and in the New Testament, Rom 4:17.

6. *Pentateuch with Targum Onkelos, Haphtaroth and Rashi's Commentary: Genesis*, 2. R. Huna in name of Bar Kappara: God created heaven and earth out of *bohu wa bohu*. GenR 2–3.

beginning of everything," making God create the heavens and the earth out of nothing. But, the text portrays watery waste as primordial and God fashioning an ordered and livable environment for living creatures and the human race. "The point of creation is not the production of matter out of nothing, but rather the emergence of a stable community in a benevolent and life-sustaining order."[7]

The heavens and the earth. This contrasting pair stands for the universe and is meant to indicate all that exists. Obviously the biblical writer was speaking of his experience of our cosmic system, though his confession of faith would include other constellations had he known of their existence. *And the earth was without form or shape [tohu wa-bohu], with darkness over the abyss.* The picture is that of water everywhere shrouded in darkness, just as in the creation myths of Israel's neighbors. *Tehom* (abyss) appears often in the Hebrew Bible, never with the definite article, always as the deeps. There may be oblique reference to Tiamat, the salt-water deity that the creating god, Marduk, overcame and split into two, the waters above and waters below. However, in our text, *Tehom* is just a watery mass, no personification, no combat.

And a mighty wind sweeping over the waters. I discussed this phrase in the last chapter. The meaning of the subject and the verb is uncertain. *Ruah* means wind, breath, spirit, depending on context. *Ruah elohīm* literally means "a wind/breath of God," but the relationship between the two nouns needs be determined. *Elohīm* (God, god, or gods) can be used as superlative qualifier to refer to the height, greatness, or grandeur of something. And so translations vary.

- And a wind from God sweeping over the water, TNK
- While a wind from God swept over the face of the waters, NRSV
- And a mighty wind sweeping over the waters, NABRE
- With a divine wind sweeping over the waters, NJB
- And the spirit of God hovered over the surface of the water, REB
- And the Spirit of God was hovering over the waters, NIV

The NIV Christianizes the text; by writing "Spirit of God" (Spirit in capital) it alludes to a creating action of the Holy Spirit. The root of the verb *merahephet* occurs again only in Deut 32:11 and there it refers to an eagle

---

7. Levenson, *Creation and the Persistence of Evil*, 12. See also Blenkinsopp, *Creation, Un-Creation, Re-Creation*, 31.

hovering or fluttering over its nest. For the waters of the flood, Gen 8:1 referred to the action of wind: "God made a wind sweep [ya☒abar ruah— caused a wind to cross] over the earth, and the waters [of the flood] began to subside."

Then God said: let there be light, and there was light. God saw that the light was good. Creation by word, though not unique to Israel, shows the creator's absolute power and might. The same word of God in the mouth of prophets controls history and the destiny of individuals and peoples. God is also said to *"make"* and *"separate"* things, but the pervasive note is that of creation by word. Nothing opposed God or stood in the way of God's intentions (but see below for other biblical traditions of God's combat against primordial forces). The light on the first day cannot proceed from the luminaries created on the fourth day. The creation myths also had light and luminaries in the same order. Isaiah 60:19–20 prophesied for Zion, the City of God, the return of the light of the first three days: "no longer shall the sun be your light by day, nor shall the brightness of the moon give you light by night; rather, the Lord will be your light forever." The rabbis saw this light stored up for the righteous in the messianic future.[8] Rev 21:23 says of the Jerusalem from above that "the city had no need of sun or moon to shine on it, for the glory of God gave it light, and its lamp was the Lamb." *Good* relates to God's purpose in creating; the structure makes it clear that God is preparing a habitat for his creatures. Everything is *good* (*very good*, v. 31); evil enters the stage only in Genesis 3 and that due to human fault. However, the darkness that preceded creation was not eliminated, only confined to night and alternates with day. The formless abyss, another primordial force, is held in check above and below; but the cataclysm of the flood shows how precarious this can be. Israel's poetic tradition contains many references to the ancient creation combat motif[9]

---

8. b. Hag 12a. See also *GenR* 3:6.

9. For example, God's battle with the Sea, Rahab, Leviathan, Dragon, Thanninim. They now only serve to highlight the absolute power of Israel's God. Ps 74:1–14, "Yet, you, God, are my king from of old, winning victories throughout the earth. You stirred up the sea by your might; you smashed the heads of the dragons on the waters. You crushed the heads of Leviathan, gave him as food to the sharks." Ps 89:11, "You crush Rahab with a mortal blow; with your strong arm you scatter your foes." Ps 104:7–9, "At your rebuke they [the deeps] took flight, at the sound of your thunder they fled. They rushed up the mountains, down the valleys to the place you had fixed for them." Isa 51:9–11, "Was it not you who crushed Rahab, you who pierced the dragon? Was it not you who dried up the sea into a way for the redeemed to pass through?" Isa 27:1 transposes this combat to "on that day."

and bewails the periodic surging of the forces of chaos in historical events and personages that threaten to submerge creation and God's people. Such appear especially in communal laments in which God's mighty deeds of the past are recalled. God's complete mastery over the universe and forces of history is thus not always apparent in historical experience and people of faith have to grapple with the problem of evil and the seeming absence of God. Isaiah 45:7 merely reaffirmed God's absolute sovereignty: *I form the light, and create the darkness, I make weal and create woe*. For this Isaiah text, God is all powerful, good and evil are subject to him. He can send Israel to exile, but also crush empires and redeem his people. Isaiah 51:9–11 has recourse to the power of prayer, invoking God's faithfulness and power: "Awake, awake, put on strength, arm of the Lord! Awake as in the days of old, in ages long ago!" Job's experience belies the facile solution that all evil is due to human sin.

> Where evil is only of human origin, suffering is to be attributed only to sin . . . But in the Hebrew Bible, it is possible . . . to fault God himself for the suffering and to dare him to act as the magisterial world-orderer that the old myth celebrates. This implies that more than just human repentance is necessary if life is to be just and God is really to rule.[10]

God's people in due course found a solution in a figure called Satan[11] who was initially a member of the divine council (Job 1–2; Zech 3:1–2; 1 Chr 21:1), but became a divine adversary in the intertestamental period (Wisd 2:24: by the envy of the Devil, death entered the world and they who are allied with him experience it).

Evening came, and morning followed—the first day. Even today in the State of Israel, the day begins at sunset. A remnant of this Jewish practice is seen in the practice of the First Vespers of Sundays and Solemnities.

10. Levenson, *Creation and the Persistence of Evil*, 49.
11. Amit, *Hidden Polemics*, 13.

Biblical conception of the world: (1) waters above the firmament;
(2) storehouses of snows; (3) storehouses for hail; (4) chambers of
winds; (5) firmament; (6) sluice; (7) pillars of the sky; (8) pillars of the
earth; (9) fountain of the deep; (10) navel of the earth; (11) waters
under the earth; (12) rivers of the nether world.

Figure 1

*Let there be a dome in the middle of the waters to separate one body of
water from the other . . . And so it happened.* The figure above[12] portrays the
ancient understanding of the cosmos on which our narrative is based. The
sky is conceived as a solid shield into which are fixed sluices for rain water.
And so it happened and has remained for all time. Cassuto[13] underlines the
durative value of *kēn*, established, firmly set. Twice the verb *hībdīl*, to separate, occurs. The concept of separation is dear to Priestly theology, for example, Israel must separate herself from Gentiles. Holiness and wholeness

12. Borrowed from Sarna, *Understanding Genesis*, 5.
13. Cassuto, *Commentary on the Book of Genesis*, 1:32.

consist in not mixing genres, separating what should not go together, assigning things their proper category, and assessing their fitness.[14]

Let the earth bring forth vegetation: every kind of plant that bears seed and every kind of fruit tree on earth that bears fruit with its seed in it. Plants and fruit trees came forth with an inbuilt power of reproduction. They do not need a further blessing to increase and multiply. The fertility rites practiced by pagan peoples are both mistaken and useless; God is the only source of fertility and fruitfulness. We note that God associates the earth as an agent with his act of creation, just as he will soon command the earth to bring forth animals. What all this might mean for scientific ideas of evolution will be briefly touched upon in the appendix.

God made the two great lights, the greater one to govern the day, and the lesser one to govern the night, and the stars. It is not entirely clear how there were evenings and mornings without the luminaries. Rashi opines that the luminaries had been created on the first day, but suspended in the firmament on the fourth day.[15] Sailhamer translates the Hebrew: "let the lights in the expanse be for separating . . ."[16] That is, the lights were already in the firmament from the first day; on the fourth they were given a new purpose, namely, to separate day and night. Cassuto opines that "God caused light to shine upon the earth from some other source without recourse to the sun; but when he created the luminaries he handed over to them the task of separation."[17] It seems that the writer did not bother about this matter since the same order of light and luminaries occurred also in ancient myths of creation. *Shemesh* and *Yareaḥ* (sun and moon) were gods in cultures around Israel. Astral cults spread with the Assyrian Empire (900–600 BCE); the stars were deemed to control destiny. Not only are these not named, they are assigned to mark times for the worship of God and to serve the good of humankind and creation. To govern, *limshōl*, is language of rule; the ancients believed that the heavenly bodies were animate.

God created the great sea monsters . . . and God blessed them, saying: be fertile and multiply, and fill the water of the seas; and let the birds multiply on the earth. The use of *bara'*, create, seems intentionally to designate a new order of being, living beings; this verb will also be used shortly of animals

14. Cf. Levenson, *Creation and the Persistence of Evil,* 127.

15. *Pentateuch with Targum Onkelos, Haphtaroth and Rashi's Commentary: Genesis,* 5.

16. Sailhamer, *Pentateuch as Narrative,* 93.

17. Cassuto, *Commentary on the Book of Genesis,* 1:44.

and humans. *Tannīnīm* (sea monsters) were among primordial adversaries of God in poetic texts. Job 7:12 complained to God, "am I the Sea, or the dragon (*tannīn*) that you place a watch over me?" Here, however, the sea monsters are merely creatures of God. Blessing, the power to increase and be successful, appears for the first time with living beings. It is both a charge and a task: "in the first sense, blessing charges the recipient with a special kind of energy or force; in the second sense, the blessing charges the recipient with a task and a responsibility."[18]

Then God said: let the earth bring forth every kind of living creature . . . God made every kind of wild animal, every kind of tame animal and every kind of thing that crawls on the ground. On the sixth day, God made animals and human beings, both having life-blood in them. The command is given the earth to bring forth the animals, but God himself made them. Did the earth produce stuff that God molded, as would happen in Genesis 2? Beasts, like human beings, are living beings with life blood in them; all life is presented as directly dependent upon God.

Then God said: let us make human beings in our image, after our likeness. Let them have dominion over the fish of the sea, the birds of the air . . . God created mankind in his image; in the image of God he created them; male and female he created them. The consultation and the verb *barā⊠* indicate a new level of being. Humankind is characterized as *zākār ûneqēbah*, biological, not sociological terms, male and female, not man and wife;[19] hence concern here is with procreation and the permanence of the species. They are created in one swoop; nothing about the female being created from the male. Both male and female are like God and in his image;[20] but is the godhead also male and female? In contrast to the surrounding cultures, Israel never entertained sexuality in her God. Whom does God address when he says, "*let us*," and why after saying "our *likeness*" did God create mankind "*in* his *image*"? Some scholars find here self-exhortation or the plural of majesty. However, all through the Hebrew Bible, God does have a council. "See! The man has become like one of us, knowing good and evil" (Gen 3:22). "Whom shall I send and who will go for us?" (Isa 6:8) Here the presence of seraphim is specifically noted. At creation, "the morning stars sang together and all the sons of God shouted for joy" (Job 38:7).

18. Mann, *Book of the Torah* (2013), 21.

19. Bird, "Genesis I–III," 33.

20. 1 Cor 10:7, "a man . . . is the image and glory of God, but woman is the glory of man," is clearly not derived from Gen 1.

Some scholars think that ṣelem, image/statue, and demut, likeness, mean roughly the same thing; others that "in our likeness" softens the plasticity of "in our own image." Anyway, both terms appear in Gen 5:3: at the age of a hundred and thirty, Adam fathered a son in his likeness, after his image. The meaning is physical resemblance—Seth was physically like Adam. So also in our text: human beings are as related to God as Seth was to Adam, though this resemblance is not through physical generation. They are like the benē Elohim, sons of God, who share likeness with God.[21] In the Yahwistic account of creation (Genesis 2:4b—3:24), the human attempt to be like God is hubris, punished with the setting up of boundaries between the divine and the human realms, and finally with expulsion from the garden (Gen 3:22). In Babylon, the luminaries and stars are seen as the "likeness" of the gods, endowed with personality, mind, and will.[22] For the Priestly writer, God created humankind to be like him. In light of the prohibition of all images, this saying is very significant, human beings disclose something of the very nature of God. The idea of likeness to God did not go unchallenged in the Hebrew Bible. Second Isaiah, the prophet of the exile, insisted on the absolute incomparability of God: "to whom can you liken God? With what likeness can you confront him?" (Isa 40:18; see also 40:25; 46:5). He seems even to deny that God consulted anyone: "who had directed the spirit of the Lord, or instructed him as his counselor? Whom did he consult to gain knowledge?" (Isa 40:13–14).[23]

It is best to separate image from likeness, they function differently in the context. Being in the image indicates an honor and task given to humankind—dominion over what God created. Rather than human beings being created for the relief of the gods as in the myths, God created everything for the sake of human beings, the world as a place where God can dwell with them as in a sanctuary. The Priestly writer presents humankind as the only replica and representative of God on earth.[24] In Egyptian court style, the Pharaoh is often called "image of Re," the god calls him "my living image." These terms designate him as viceroy or representative of the god on earth, with something of divinity present in him. Some scholars see in Gen 1 a democratization of this royal attribute which is now transferred to all human beings—every person is royalty. Because human beings are

21. Miller, Genesis 1–11, 20.

22. Cassuto, Commentary on the Book of Genesis, 1:43.

23. Cf. Levenson, Creation and the Persistence of Evil, 124.

24. Blenkinsopp, Creation, Uncreation, Recreation, 28.

theomorphic,[25] to see a human person is to be presented with something of God. Westermann[26] thinks that such a view is foreign to the Priestly writer whose theology is dominated by God's holiness, a God who reveals himself only at the holy place. He states that God appears in God's *kabōd* (glory) as a manifestation before human beings, not in human beings. With Karl Barth, he would rather see the "image of God" as categorizing human beings in their ability to enter into relationship with God. He thus writes that "human [beings] are created in such a way that their very existence is intended to be their relationship to God."[27] But this reasoning about the Priestly writer and *kabōd* can be countered by the fact that in Ps 8:5 God crowned human beings with glory and majesty (*kabōd we-hadar*), attributes of God, and derivatively of the king. In so doing, God aligned them to the divine realm, making them only "little less than a god," or in the translation of the NRSV "a little lower than God." The faith of Israel speaks here of humanity as such. The nations share with Israel this image and likeness to God that is more fundamental than Israel's particular election. God calls Israel "my firstborn son" (Exod 4:23), but Israel is not alone in the fundamental likeness to God and the inherent demand to live according to the pattern of God, to imitate God.

As "image," human beings are to fill the earth and subdue it (Gen 1:28) and tread down the fish of the sea, the birds of heaven, the cattle and wild animals (Gen 1:26). The verbs *radah* (trample down) and *kabash* (subdue) are usual for royal subjection of enemies. In Gen 9:2, God's blessing of human beings makes the terror and dread of them fall upon the animal kingdom now given into human hands. The earth was created in "frontier" state, and human beings under God are to "green" the earth and beautify it. As "image of God" they are viceroys of the creator on earth. God had already created everything according to its kind, with inherent laws proper to each. These laws will serve human beings as blueprint for their nurturing of creation. Nothing is said here about ruling or subduing fellow human beings—every human being is royalty. We are thus left with a double divine commission—to humanity and to Israel, the one serving the other: "Gen 1–11 concerns the affirmation that God calls the world into being to be

25. Rad, *Commentary on Genesis*, 145.

26. Westermann, *Genesis 1–11*, 153.

27. Ibid., 158.

his faithful world . . . Gen 12–50 concerns the affirmation that God calls a special people to be faithfully his people."[28]

The Jewish and Christian faiths have come to the realization that Scripture gives no warrant to humankind for unlimited exploitation of the earth, but rather to shepherd it, just as the earth shepherds us. As such, ecologists now prefer the term "mutual custodianship."[29] The language of "rule/subdue" is to be understood in terms of mutual nurturing, for in our ecosystem, all beings are interconnected and the good of one is the good of all. Pope Francis insists,

> We are not God. The earth was here before us and it has been given to us. This allows us to respond to the charge that Judeo-Christian thinking, on the basis of the Genesis account which grants man "dominion" over the earth (cf. Gen 1:28), has encouraged the un-bridled exploitation of nature by painting him as domineering and destructive by nature. This is not a correct interpretation of the Bible as understood by the Church . . . In our time, the Church does not simply state that other creatures are completely subor-dinated to the good of human beings, as if they have no worth in themselves and can be treated as we wish.[30]

God also said: see, I give you every seed-bearing plant on all the earth. God's original intention is that *nephesh hayyah* (a living creature, that is, animals and humans) will not kill nor be killed for food, but rather eat greens and fruits. That means respect for all life, even that of animals. The flood will result from the corruption of the earth in that "the earth is full of *hamas* because of them" (Gen 6:13). *Hamas* means violence, even wan-ton violence. From the rearrangements after the flood, we deduce that this included slaughter of life. Animals and human beings abandoned God's dispensation on the matter. Isaiah 11:7 promises a return to the beginnings in the ideal time of Israel's salvation: "the cow and the bear shall graze . . . the lion shall eat hay like the ox." In other words, "they shall not harm or destroy on all my holy mountain," a promise recalled in Isa 65:25. A later text adds color to this: "Wild beasts shall come from the forest and minister to humans, and asps and dragons shall come out of their holes to submit themselves to a little child" (2 Bar 73:6, ca. 100 CE). All of this echoes the human longing for a return to universal peace and harmony, already voiced

28. Brueggemann, *Genesis*, 1.

29. Habel and Trudinger, *Exploring Ecological Hermeneutics*, 2.

30. Pope Francis, *Laudato Si'*, nos. 67, 69.

in the Paradise Myth of Enki and Ninhursag: "In Dilmun, the raven utters no cries, the lion kills not, the wolf snatches not the lamb, unknown is the kid-devouring wild dog."[31]

God looked at everything he had made and found it very good. In omitting evil is Genesis 1 opposing other works that emphasize the evil of human experience of creation or elevating a vision of hope in response to Israel's experience of trauma?[32] Smith also wonders whether such presentation might mean that "good" does not refer to moral good, rather benefit or well-being balancing *tohu wa-bohu*.[33] We ask, *very good* for what? "The heavens belong to the Lord, but he has given the earth to the children of Adam" (Ps 115:16). "You have given him rule over the works of your hands, put all things at his feet" (Ps 8:7). "If humans were last to enter the world— and in such a way to honor God's handiwork with God's image—is this not marvelous? It is like saying that as a king he prepared the palace and then, as king, when everything was already prepared, led in the procession."[34] Yet, a certain balance need be kept: "God created everything for man, but man in turn was created to serve and love God and to offer all creation back to him."[35] In recent times, we reckon with the fact that other living beings have a value of their own in God's eyes:

> We can speak of the priority of *being* over that of *being useful* . . . Each creature possesses its own particular goodness and perfection . . . Each of the various creatures, willed in its own being, reflects in its own way a ray of God's infinite wisdom and goodness. Man must therefore respect the particular goodness of every creature, to avoid any disordered use of things.[36]

On the seventh day God completed the work he had been doing; he rested on the seventh day [wa-yishbot ba-yōm ha-shebī'ī] *from all the work he had undertaken. God blessed the seventh day and made it holy, because on it he rested from all the work* [kī bō shabat mi-kol mela'ktō] *he had done in creation.* Did God work on the seventh day? LXX corrects to say "and on the sixth day God finished his works" in line with the correction already in Exod 31:17: "for in six days the LORD made the heavens and the earth, but

31. *ANET*, 38.

32. Smith, *Priestly Vision of Genesis 1*, 63–64.

33. Ibid., 62.

34. Gregory of Nazianzus, *Homilies on Genesis*, 44, in ACCS, 44–45.

35. *Catechism of the Catholic Church*, no. 358.

36. Pope Francis, *Laudato Si'*, no. 69.

on the seventh day he rested at his ease." "He rested on the seventh day" intends to qualify the phrase "on the seventh day God completed the work he had been doing." "From what toil did God rest? . . . So what toil could there have been for God to speak one word a day?"[37] Our narrative submerges creation through making and separating in creation through word alone. The poetic texts, as already mentioned, betray acquaintance with creation through considerable exertion: "you spread out the heavens like a tent, setting the beams of your chambers upon the waters . . . you fixed the earth on its foundation so it can never be shaken" (Ps 104:2, 5). They even spoke of combat: "you crush Rahab with a mortal blow, with your strong arm you scatter your foes" (Ps 89:11). Be that as it may, the idea of God resting seems to have garnered some opposition. Isaiah 40:28, "the . . . creator of the ends of the earth does not faint or grow weary," may be another Second Isaiah counterpoint to the Priestly writer's image of God ceasing from his work, resting and being refreshed on the seventh day.[38]

The best explanation of the "gap" created by use of the word "*rest*" is attained by reference to the Babylonian myth of creation, *Enuma Elish*. Consequent upon Marduk's victory over Tiamat, the gods decided to build him the palace/temple of Esagila as place of rest:

> Now, O lord, thou who hast caused our deliverance, what shall be our homage to thee? Let us build a shrine whose name shall be called "Lo, a chamber for our nightly rest"; let us repose in it! Let us build a throne, a recess for his abode![39]

"Rest" means that everything is under control. Marduk's sovereignty is now unchallenged and will remain so. So he hung his no-longer-needed bow in the sky. The order established by him will continue indefinitely. In light of this background, the rest of God in Gen 2:2 is a declaration of sovereignty over the world that God has created.[40] In the Babylonian creation myth, Marduk's sovereignty means the foundation and supremacy of Babylon. Creation in Genesis 1 happens in "no place"—no spot on earth can claim primordiality. The account ends with Sabbath, hallowed for all humanity.[41]

---

37. Ephrem the Syrian, in ACCS, 45–46.

38. Weinfeld, "God the Creator in Genesis 1," 122–26; cited in Levenson, *Creation and the Persistence of Evil*, 124.

39. *ANET*, 68; *Enuma Elish* in the translation of E. A. Speiser.

40. Okoye, *Israel and the Nations*, 30.

41. Cf. Levenson, "Universal Horizon," 146–47.

Twice the verbal root *shabat* appears: "he *rested* on the seventh day," and "he *rested* from all the work." When Exod 20:11 cites our passage, it renders "and he *rested* on the seventh day" using the root *nuaḥ* (to rest). Exodus 31:17 makes it clearer by saying that on the seventh day the Lord "rested and drew breath," that is, refreshed himself. The emphasis on rest is a subtle allusion to the Sabbath and its rest. A cycle of time that ends with rest every seventh day was an innovation in the ancient world. The innovation is established and sanctioned by God who at creation blessed the seventh day and made it holy. Legislation details what the rest of God means for Israel.

> Six days you may labor and do all your work, but the seventh day is a Sabbath of the LORD your God. You shall not do any work, either you, your son or your daughter, your male or female slave, your work animal, or the resident alien within your gates. (Exod 20:9–10)

Every living thing, human or beast, will rest on the seventh day, and that as a "Sabbath of the LORD, your God." When our text writes the Sabbath into the very constitution of the cosmos, this makes it part of God's sovereignty to grant a share of his own relief and refreshment to all, beast and human, Israelite and non-Israelite, slave or free. Our text lays the foundation for the precept of the Sabbath. The sanctity of Sabbath is older than Israel and rests on all humankind as established by *Elohim*, the common God of all.[42] It proclaims the lordship of God over all humanity as something that guarantees the welfare of everyone and everything. By God's act of setting the Sabbath apart, all human beings are gifted with a cycle of work and rest, not only masters but also slaves and animals.[43]

Hitherto blessing is spoken only of living things and portends the power of procreation and success in life. Here time is blessed: *God blessed the seventh day and made it holy*. The verbal root *qadēsh* literally means to set apart, separate from all else. The seventh day is quality time—for nurturing self and ties to the creator. Holiness was usually attributed to persons, places, and cult objects. What does it mean to hallow time, the seventh day? The later group of Priestly writers, the Holiness Group, evident especially in Leviticus 17–26, were keen on expanding the realm of holiness from cult to all of life. So in this hallowing of the seventh day,

---

42. Cassuto, *Genesis 1–11*, 63.

43. Okoye, *Israel and the Nations*, 29.

35

holiness filters down, spreads out, and dominates all areas of life . . . The Sabbath is thus transformed into a realm of expansion of holiness . . . The Israelite is cut off from time and rhythm of his environment and connected to a new understanding of time, which might be called divine time or the Holiness Calendar—a new and different pace of life.[44]

On the seventh day God completed the work. The following "conclusion formulas," all from the same Priestly writer, use a form of the verb *kalah* (to finish, complete).

- Thus the heavens and all their array were *completed* . . . God *completed* the work (Gen 2:1–2).

- Thus the entire work was *completed* . . . thus Moses *finished* all the work (Exod 39:32; 40:33).

- Thus they *finished* dividing the land (Josh 19:51).

In the theology of the Priestly writer, the created world, the tabernacle, and the land of Israel have something in common: they represent a world in perfect conformity with the designs of the creator. When the creator looked at all he had made, he saw it was very good (Gen 1:31), it contained nothing against the creator's wishes. The tabernacle was erected exactly according to a heavenly pattern shown to Moses. The promised land, symbolized by Zion, is God's chosen home, "Yes the LORD has chosen Zion, desired it for a dwelling. 'This is my resting place for ever; here I will dwell, for I desire it'" (Ps 132:13–14). The whole world, with the sign of the Sabbath over it, is meant to be a sanctuary, a place of "rest" for God, a place where God's sovereignty is acclaimed and where God may dwell with his creation. Tabernacle and temple are truly the world in microcosm. Israel bears within herself the vocation of the whole earth to be the home of God. The "*rest*" of God at creation is promise and demand: promise that God will finally come to rest in God's creation, demand that Israel function to bring all things to that rest. And as pledge of this, the Sabbath of Israel hangs over all creation.[45]

What have we come to know of God in this chapter? Elohim is majestic, creating and ordering by word and according to a plan in which everything has its place. His very first word is a command, and his commands

---

44. Amit, *Polemics*, 238–39.

45. Okoye, *Israel and the Nations*, 32.

are obeyed to the letter: let there be light—and there was light. He is transcendent, the chasm between him and humans is as deep as the heavens are from earth. Yet, he delights to dispose the environment to the best for all his creatures to thrive, makes the world a place to dwell with creatures. He takes the earth and humans into partnership, particularly humans whom he created to be like him and on whom he laid the charge of the care of the earth. Sentiments of love are not explicitly mentioned, but those of delight ("and it was good," "very good," 1:31), delight in disposing all for the good of humans and all creation. This is none other than Good diffusive of itself. It calls for a return of gratitude and self-surrender in worship.

Tradition

Jews and Christians employed similar hermeneutics, only that Christians read the Old Testament largely as witness to Christ. Because of the constraints of space, we are very selective and focus only on major distinguishing interpretive elements.

In the Beginning/Bereshīt. An important text in the debate between Jews and Christians and between the early Fathers of the church and heretics was Prov 8:22: "*the Lord begot me the beginning [reshīt] of his works.*" Wisdom speaks here. She continues: "When he established the heavens, there was I . . . when he fixed the foundations of earth, then was I beside him as artisan . . ." Wisd 9:9 goes further: "Now with you is Wisdom, who knows your works and was present when you made the world, who understands what is pleasing to you . . ." What or who is wisdom and what is its role in creation? Ben Sira 24:23 identified wisdom with Torah. Early Jewish interpreters read *be-* in *bereshīt* as "by means of" or "with the help of"[46] the Torah, hence by means of the Torah God created the world[47] or God created the world for the sake of the Torah.[48]

For Christians, wisdom and "word of God" referred to the Son. Hence, John 1:1: "*In the beginning* was the Word, and Word was with God, and the Word was God." That Word took flesh as Jesus Christ. Further reflection attached to Ps 33:6, "By the Lord's word the heavens were made; by the breath of his mouth all their host." Irenaeus of Lyons (135–202 CE) was among

---

46. Kugel, *Bible as It Was*, 56.

47. *GenR* I.1.

48. *Pentateuch with Rashi's Commentary*, 2.

the first to speak of "the two hands of God" in creation and redemption,[49] that is, the Word and the Spirit (breath of his mouth).[50] Among Christians, debate on the nature of Christ centered around Prov 8:22 and 8:25 which Christians read in the Septuagint. It had, "the Lord created me" at v. 22 and "begot" me at v. 25. Justin Martyr was the first to use this text for the origin of the Logos in God.[51] Later, the Arians fixed on the word "created" and regarded Christ as the firstfruit of God's creation, hence as a creature. Origen fixed on "begot" as primary and "created" as a generic synonym.[52]

Creation out of Nothing (creatio ex nihilo). Creation out of matter was still taught in Wisd 11:17, a Hellenistic Jewish text of the first century BCE, which says, "Not without means was your almighty hand, that had fashioned the universe from formless matter." However, about the same time a Greek text, for the first time, expressed faith in creation out of nothing. The mother of seven martyrs pleaded with her last born: "I beg you, child, to look at the heavens and the earth and see all that is in them; then you will know that God did not make them out of existing things" (2 Macc 7:28). From there on, Jewish and Christian faith have proclaimed creation out of nothing: "[God] gives life to the dead and calls into being what does not exist" (Rom 4:17); this refers to barren Sarah's conception of Isaac in her old age—a miracle that shows God's dominion of life. "By faith we understand that the universe was ordered by the word of God, so that what is visible came into being through the invisible" (Heb 11:3).

---

49. *Against Heresies*, IV, preface. See Irenaeus, "For by the hands of the Father, that is, by the Son and the Holy Spirit, man, and not [merely] a part of man, was made in the likeness of God." *Against Heresies*, V, 6.

50. Ephrem the Syrian outlined the participation of each: "the Father spoke. The Son created. And so it was also right that the Spirit offer its work, clearly shown through its hovering, in order to demonstrate its unity with the other persons. Thus we learn that all was brought to perfection and accomplished by the Trinity." *Commentary on Genesis 1*, in ACCS, 6.

51. *Dialogue with Trypho*, 61.

52. Simonetti, *Biblical Interpretation in the Early Church*, 123.

TRADITIONAL AFRICAN COSMOLOGY

God

Spirits
Living dead, animal spirits
Mystical forces

Humans and Cosmos

God and the Spirits. African traditional religion is representative of many traditional religions. Creation is the work of the Supreme Being. The spirits, though inferior in power to the Supreme Being, seem autonomous and do as they please. Most prayers are addressed to God; but most sacrifices are offered not to God, rather to the earth deity and the spirits, some of whom represent ancestors within the memory of the living (whom Mbiti calls the "living dead"). The basic worldview, adapting John Mbiti, *Introduction to African Religion*, 35, includes three orders of being (see text box). Among mystical forces, witches and witchcraft feature prominently in some places. Religious practice for many traditional Christians is a constant struggle to placate or ward off undomesticated forces of evil; salvation is often seen partly as deliverance from these. In this context, Genesis 1 proclaims the absolute sovereignty and omnipotence of God.

EPHREM, SPIRIT MAKES FERTILE WATERS OF BAPTISM

"The action of a hen is similar . . . the Holy Spirit foreshadows the sacrament of holy baptism, prefiguring its arrival, so that the waters made fertile by the hovering of that same divine Spirit might give birth to the children of God"—*ruh* is feminine. (Ephrem the Syrian, *Commentary on Genesis 1*, in ACCS, 6).

The Action of the Spirit Prefigures Christian Baptism. The LXX rendered Gen 1:2 as *pneuma theou epephereto* (the Spirit of God rushing down upon the waters). It may have been at the root of patristic typology that sees here a foreshadowing of the Spirit's action over the waters of baptism. Jerome wrote: "'The Spirit was stirring above the waters'—already at that time baptism was being foreshadowed."[53] The Catholic Liturgy of the Blessing of Baptismal Water on Holy Saturday night reflects this interpretation:

> O God, whose Spirit in the first moments of the world's creation hovered over the waters, so that the very substance of water would even then take to itself the power to sanctify. . . (Holy Saturday, Blessing of Baptismal Water)

The Image and Likeness of God. Wisd 2:23 interpreted the image of God as immortality, the essential quality of the gods: "for God formed us to be imperishable; the image of his own nature he made us." Both Jewish and early Christian tradition were anxious to deny that God was of flesh or in human form. Ambrose of Milan (333–397) articulated it this way: "Is it true that the flesh is made 'to the image of God'? In that case, is there earth in God, since flesh is of the earth? Is God corporeal? . . . The flesh, therefore, cannot be made to the image of God. This is true however of our souls, which are free to wander far and wide in acts of reflection and of counsel."[54] Origen (185–254) concurs: "But it is our inner man, invisible, incorporeal, incorruptible and immortal, that is made 'according to the image of God.'"[55] A play on words in Greek brings this out: the image of God is *Logos* (the Word, also Reason), humans are *logikos*[56] (rational, having intellect and will). In Catholic Social Teaching, being in the image and likeness of God is the very root of human dignity. In African American history, creation demonstrated the Fatherhood of God and Brotherhood of Man. Being created in the image and likeness of God assures all human beings of dignity and equality before God and humankind. In the slavery period, African Americans read the image and likeness of God as confirming their inner dignity and worth and as a basis of hope for eventual freedom.

Be Fertile and Multiply. Ancient Jewish tradition viewed this as the first mitzvah of the Torah's 613 precepts, namely the obligation incumbent on males to marry and have children.

> No man may abstain from keeping the law *Be fruitful and multiply*, unless he already has children: according to the School of Shammai, two sons; according to the School of Hillel,[57] a son and

---

53. *Homilies* 10, in ACCS, 6.

54. *Hexaemeron* 6.8.44–45, in ACCS, 32.

55. *Homilies on Genesis*, in ACCS, 31.

56. Clement of Alexandria, *Exhortation to the Greeks* 10, in ACCS, 29.

57. Hillel and Shammai thrived in the late first century BCE.

a daughter, for it is written, *Male and female created he them*. . .
The duty to be fruitful and multiply falls on the man but not on
the woman. R. Johanan b. Baroka says: *Of them both it is written, And God blessed them and God said unto them, Be fruitful and
multiply.*[58]

Jesus of Nazareth and Saul of Tarsus were both celibate, but they were Jews
under the spell of the coming kingdom of God. Under the same spell a fac-
tion in the Church of Corinth held it best for a man not to touch a woman,
that is, not to marry (1 Cor 7:1). Of Jewish rabbis, a rabbi of the second
century, Simeon ben Azzai (ca. 140 CE), is remembered as choosing celi-
bacy. His reason? "I desire to study Torah while the world can be preserved
through others."[59]

Scripture and Ecology. The Jewish and Christian faiths currently insist that Scripture gives no warranty to humankind to rape the earth. In
our ecosystem, all beings are interconnected, the good of one is the good
of all. Pope Francis insists that ecological conversion (*Laudato Si'*, no. 5)
is needed, for Christians need "realize that their responsibility within creation, and their duty toward nature and the Creator, are an essential part
of their faith."[60] For, "the ultimate purpose of other creatures is not to be
found in us. Rather, all creatures are moving forward with us and through
us toward a common point of arrival, which is God . . . Human beings . . .
are called to lead all creatures back to their Creator."[61] Among the many re-
sources available, I may mention *The Green Bible: Understanding the Bible's
Powerful Message for the Earth*, which writes in green letters all texts of
the Bible concerning the earth. There is also the Earth Bible Series with
several publications. The six guiding ecojustice principles of this series are
articulated as follows.[62]

- Principle of intrinsic worth—all earth's components have intrinsic
  value.

- Principle of interconnectedness—all are mutually dependent on each
  other for life and survival.

---

58. m. Yebamoth 6:6 in Danby, *The Mishnah*, 227.

59. *GenR* 34.14.

60. Ibid., no. 64, citing John Paul II, *Message for the 1990 World Day of Peace*, 15.

61. *Laudato Si'*, no. 83.

62. Habel, *Readings from the Perspective of Earth*, 38–53.

- Principle of voice—earth is living entity capable of raising its voice in celebration, against injustice.

- Principle of purpose—all earth's components are part of a dynamic cosmic design.

- Principle of mutual custodianship—humans as partners with, not rulers over, the earth.

- Principle of resistance—earth suffers injustice but also actively resists and struggles for justice.

The Meaning of the Sabbath. Rev 1:10 (ca. 100 CE) writes: "I was caught up in spirit on the LORD's day." We have here attestation of the Christian transfer of the Sabbath to Sunday in honor of the Lord's resurrection and the new world order created by it. The Jewish mystic, Abraham Heschel, wrote a reflection on the Sabbath. Sabbath (or the LORD's day) is a window from time looking into eternity.

> The meaning of the Sabbath is to celebrate time rather than space. Six days a week we live under the tyranny of things of space; on the Sabbath we try to become attuned to holiness in time. It is a day on which we are called upon to share in what is eternal in time, to turn from the results of creation to the mystery of creation.[63]

Appendix: Creation and Evolution[64]

Faith and reason are grounded in the same God; believers thus adopt the attitude of *fides quaerens intellectum* (faith seeking understanding). The import of Genesis 1 is not to tell us how the heavens go but how to go to heaven (St. Augustine). The author of Genesis 1 held a dialogue of faith with the traditional knowledge of the time. We are called upon to dialogue with the scientific knowledge of our time: "science offers the best available knowledge of how the world operates. Theology offers a vision of value, meaning, and hope."[65] Saint Pope John Paul II wrote, "Science can purify religion from error and superstition; religion can purify science from idolatry and

---

63. Heschel, *Sabbath*, 10.

64. I acknowledge dependence on Hayes, *Gift of Being*. I have also consulted Ratzinger, "*In the Beginning. . .*"; Fleming, *Truth about Science and Religion*.

65. Hayes, *Gift of Being*, 18.

false absolutes."[66] Science and faith however have their areas of competence and their methods. A point of possible tension is that the Bible focuses on *who* creates, science details *how* the universe came to be and *how long* the process took.[67] Genesis 1 posits a creator from outside the system, science seeks answers from within the universe and does not reckon with a creator outside the system.

There has been development of doctrine, and scientific theories have also evolved through time. Most people no longer believe that our world is about 6,000 years old, as the Bible seems to posit. Science postulates that planet earth formed about four billion years ago, and that the universe possibly originated about 13.7 billion years ago. The biblical writer's experience was of our constellation; science continues to discover numerous constellations beside which ours is less than a speck of dust. No longer do we see the universe as geocentric as in the biblical text, rather as heliocentric, revolving around the sun. On October 31, 1992, Saint John Paul II lifted the condemnation of Galileo who was condemned for the "heresy" of heliocentrism.

Genesis 1 nevertheless questions the autogenesis of the universe or that matter is eternal, for "in the beginning God created the heavens and the earth." It postulates that "God is the reason that the world exists. It is not self-sufficient or *causa sui*."[68] However, there are hints of processes. God commanded the earth to bring forth vegetation (Gen 1:11). How long did the waters take to be gathered together so as to let dry land appear? There was creative progression:[69] let the earth produce living creatures according to their kinds" (Gen 1:24). In the case of plants and fruit trees, the earth brought them forth with seed already implanted in them for self-reproduction.

> [Creation] did not spring forth complete from the hands of the Creator. The universe was created "in a state of journeying" (*in statu viae*) toward an ultimate perfection yet to be attained, to which God destined it.[70]

---

66. Letter to Rev. George V. Coyne, Director of the Vatican Observatory, June 1, 1988.
67. Fleming, *Truth about Science and Religion*, 26.
68. Fergusson, "Interpreting the Story of Creation," 158.
69. Fleming, *Truth about Science and Religion*, 24.
70. *Catechism of the Catholic Church*, no. 302.

The quasi-identity of cellular chemistry throughout the biosphere needs explanation. At the microscopic level, human beings are composed of elements of the universe. Whatever theory is adduced to account for the observed scientific phenomena, the big bang, quantum physics, development of the species, faith posits a creator originating and presiding over the organization of the cosmos—a process initiated and directed by God.

As to evolutionary biology, in whatever manner the species developed, "the Catholic faith obliges us to hold that souls are immediately created by God."[71]

71. Pius XII, *Humani generis.*

CHAPTER 3

Genesis 2:4b—3:24

The Story of the Garden

> *The Lord is gracious and merciful,*
> *slow to anger and abounding in mercy.*

—PSALM 145:8

Introduction

The reader pauses at 2:4b,[1] *when the LORD God made the earth and the heavens*, for a new story[2] seems to begin here. The earlier focus was on the heavens (*the heavens and the earth*), now the focus is on the earth (*the earth and the heavens*). The order, the earth and the heavens, recurs in the Hebrew Bible only in Ps 148:13. Elohim (God), the deity in the first story, is replaced by YHWH Elohim (LORD God). The coupling of YHWH and Elohim points to the identity of Elohim of Genesis 1 with YHWH of Genesis 4.[3] The phrase is remarkably lacking in the dialogue of the snake and the woman, Gen 3:1–5, which consistently uses Elohim.

---

1. Following NRSV; NABRE starts the unit at 2:4a ("this is the story of the heavens and the earth . . .). Most scholars attribute the unit that runs till 3:24 to the Yahwist.

2. Traditional Jewish exegesis and some Fathers of the Church see the events of Gen 2–3 as mere elaborations of the sixth day of creation in Gen 1. A significant number of Jewish exegetes, though, accept that here we have two differently conceived accounts of creation.

3. Outside Gen 2–3, YHWH Elohim recurs in the Pentateuch only in Exod 9:30, in the Latter Prophets only in Jonah 4:6. It appears once each in Samuel and Kings (2 Sam

The *style* is different: Elohim was majestic and transcendent, creating by word, YHWH Elohim is immanent, fumbles, molds a figure, plants a garden, and strolls in the garden in the cool of the day. The first story is characterized by repetitive and formulaic language; here there is true narration, the story develops through the interaction of the characters involved. Many scholars speak of the Priestly story of creation (Genesis 1) and the Yahwist story of Eden (Genesis 2:4b—3:24).

PURPOSE OF GENESIS 2–3

The primary purpose of the Torah in these chapters is to explain how it is that in the Lord's world, the world of the good and beneficent God, evil should exist and man should endure pain and troubles and calamities . . . man corrupts it by his conduct and brings evil into the world as a result of his corruption . . . other lessons from this section: we learn of the necessity of discipline founded on God's statutes; of man's innate conscience; of the law of divine reward and punishment; of the bonds of brotherhood uniting the inhabitants of the world . . . of the humane treatment that we should accord to animals ...of the value of marriage; of the importance of monogamy; of the humility with which it behoves us to conduct ourselves, seeing we are dust and unto dust we return . . . (Cassuto, *From Adam to Noah*, 71).

There is difference also in *content*. Genesis 1 is a cosmogony, it accounts for the world as we know it; here the focus is on humankind with no effort to account for all the world of experience (fish are not even mentioned, for example). In Genesis 1, the problem was water everywhere (suits the Babylonian background); here the problem is drought, lack of rain (as happens periodically in Palestine). Elohim commanded the earth and it brought forth the living creatures (1:24), here YHWH God formed out of the ground all the wild animals and all the birds of the air (2:19).[4] In Gen 1:25 birds were created from the waters, but in 2:19 from the earth. In

---

7:25; 2 Kgs 19:19), six times each in Chronicles and the Psalms.

4. R. Johanan ben Zakkai (reorganized Jewish scholarship after Jerusalem fell to Rome in 70 CE) was asked to clarify this and he replied that the earlier verse referred to creation, this latter of gathering them together to name them. *GenR* 17. 4.

the first story, humankind was created after the environment was already in place; here man came first, plants and animals after. In Gen 1:27 we read, "male and female he created them," that is, in one fell swoop; here creation is sequential—first the man, then the woman fashioned from his ribs. YHWH God of 3:18 seems to work at cross purposes[5] with Elohim's expressed desires in 1:19—in the former, hard labor yields thorns and thistles, here every seed-bearing plant and tree is food for man. The mandate of humankind in Gen 2:15 in respect of creatures and the earth is different from that in Gen 1:26–28: in the one, *'abad* and *shamar*, care for and conserve; in the other, *radah* and *kabash*, rule and subdue.[6]

The stories are thus discrete, lacking a follow through from the first creation account to the other. Analysis suggests that the first story intends to update the theology of the second, especially as concerns the image of God: "Genesis 2–3 offers a 'parodic revision' or doubling of Genesis 1."[7]

Structure

The story begins with the "when . . . then"[8] structure of ancient myths of creation: when nothing of the world as known existed *for the LORD God had sent no rain on the earth and there was no man to till the ground*, then YHWH God formed the man out of the dust of the ground (2:7). Jerome T. Walsh[9] finds the story organized as a chiasm of seven scenes, as follows.

5. Humphreys, *Character of God*, 48.

6. Habel, *Ecological Reading of Genesis 1–11*, 53.

7. Humphreys, *Character of God*, 52, citing Whedbee, *Bible and the Comic Vision*, 25–41.

8. The Babylonian myth of creation, *Enuma Elish* ("when on high") begins as follows: When on high the heaven had not been named, Firm ground below had not been called by name . . . No reed hut had been matted, no marsh land had appeared. . . When no gods whatever had been brought into being . . . Then it was that the gods were formed within them. . . (*ANET*, 60–61).

9. Walsh, "Gen 2:4b—3:24," 169–71.

TABLE 2: JEROME T. WALSH

Scene 1: 2:4b–17, *narrative* YHWH God speaks, man passive Settlement in garden	Scene 7: 3:22–24 *narrative* YHWH God speaks, man passive Exile back to *adamah*
Scene 2: 2:18–25, *narrative* YHWH God active (man, woman, animals passive) [ease of eating]	Scene 6: 3:14–19, *monologue* YHWH God speaks, (snake, man, woman passive) pain in eating
Scene 3: 3:1–5, *dialogue* Snake and woman theme is eating Three statements of snake	Scene 5: 3:9–13, *dialogue* YHWH God, man, woman theme is eating Three questions and answers initiated by God
Scene 4: 3:6–8, *narrative* Woman and man (God absent) Center: *wayy 'kal*, 3:6 (and she ate)	

This structure is impressive, however, other structures are possible. Having the center at 3:6 ("and she ate,") casts the whole in terms of sin and punishment. This may be too constricting, as other themes are also at play. We attend to the narrative flow, allowing it full freedom to signify.

The story moves from *ha-adamah* (the ground) to the garden of Eden, to exile from Eden, and back to *ha-adamah*. The link between the garden of Eden and the land promised to the patriarchs is suggested by the similarity of the borders of Eden in Gen 2:10–14 to those of Gen 15:18 (from the Wadi of Egypt to the Great River, the Euphrates).[10] The Israelite reader may perceive the garden of Eden as metaphor for the promised land, its loss as portraying the exile.

The Rivers of Eden

Genesis 2:10–14 is an insertion; we treat it first. *A stream ('ed) was welling up out of the earth and watering the whole surface of the ground* (Gen 2:6), parallels *a river (nahar) rises in Eden to water the garden* (Gen 2:10), then

10. Cf. Sailhamer, *Pentateuch as Narrative*, 99. Rabbi Abbahu, an Amora of the third generation (290–320 CE) makes the connection: "Just as I led Adam into the garden of Eden and commanded him, and he transgressed my commandment, whereupon I punished him by dismissal and expulsion, and bewailed him with *ekah* . . . so also did I bring his descendants into Eretz Israel and command them, and they transgressed my commandment and I punished them by sending them away and expelling them, and I bewailed them with *ekah.*" *GenR* 19. 9.

branching into four rivers that water the *oikumene*. That the river flows out of Eden to water the garden suggests that the garden was outside Eden, but in 2:8 the LORD God planted a garden *in* Eden. The unit speaks of the garden of Eden, but Ezek 28:13 equates Eden and the garden of God ("you were in Eden, the garden of God"). The trees of Eden parallel the trees in the garden of God (Ezek 31:9). Eden stands for a well-watered and fruitful land—in Gen 13:10 the Jordan plain is said to be well watered like the garden of the Lord.

The parallels with Ezekiel suggest an underlying myth of Eden, a well-watered place with lush gardens. Umberto Cassuto[11] compares the use of the myth in Ezekiel and Genesis. In both, the garden is in Eden, contains miraculous trees, cherubs are mentioned, the creature who dwelt in the garden sinned and was expelled (*Adam* in Genesis, the *cherub* in Ezekiel). Differences include the following. Ezekiel's garden of God is situated on a mountain sacred to God, though for the rivers of the Genesis account to flow into all the known areas of earth they must have originated from some high point, presumably a mountain. The location is thus not only "garden" of God, but also mountain of God: the source of living water.[12] The rivers recall the vivifying waters streaming from the temple/mountain of God (cf. Ezek 47:1–12) and thus "assert that the gift of life for all creation comes from the garden, only as gift of God."[13] The banished being in Ezekiel is the cherub (symbol for the king of Tyre) driven from God's mountain and cast down to earth, but in Genesis, the banished is *ha-adam*. In Ezekiel, precious stones and gold are found in the garden and formed the covering of the cherub; Genesis displaces these metals to the land of Havilah.

Havilah is among the descendants of Cush in the line of Ham (Gen 10:7), but among those of Joktan in the line of Shem (Gen 10:29). Saul routed Amalek from Havilah to the approaches of Shur on the frontier of Egypt (1 Sam 15:7). We may place Havilah in the southern desert region from the borders of Egypt to the Persian Gulf. Pishon is unknown; it occurs elsewhere only in Ben Sira 24:25, with Tigris, Euphrates, and Gihon as here, but also Jordan and the Nile, as illustrating the Law as overflowing with

11. *From Adam to Noah*, 73–83. See also "Excursus: Eden," in Westermann, *Genesis 1–11*, 209–10.

12. Habel, *Ecological Reading of Genesis 1–11*, 52. See also Blenkinsopp, *Creation, Uncreation, Recreation*, 61.

13. Brueggemann, *Genesis*, 46.

wisdom. Josephus identifies it with the Ganges.[14] Gihon is said to wind all through the land of Cush. Cush is usually Ethiopia, hence Gihon would be the Nile, unless Cush here refers to a location in southern Mesopotamia (1 Chr 1:9). It is hardly the tiny stream of Gihon in Jerusalem, unless the narrative intention is to magnify it as one of the life-giving waters of earth. The last two rivers, Tigris and Euphrates, are well known, as is Asshur; these root the account in history. Besides reusing elements of the myth of the garden of God, the insertion of 2:10–14 functions to point ahead to the panorama in Genesis 10.

The Story of the Garden

An *'ed*[15] wells up out of the earth to irrigate the whole surface of the ground, that is, the whole earth. The narrator does not say that the Lord God caused this flow, nor is it explicitly related to the river that rises in Eden to water the garden (2:10). The Lord God formed (using the verb *yaṣar*, to mold as a potter) *ha-adam* out of *ha-adamah*. *Ha-adam*, the man, is both individual and collective at this stage. The pun of *adam* and *adamah* points to a being of earth; *adamah* (ground, earth) is the human environment, the context of his work and sustenance, his final destiny.[16] *The man became a living being*. Living being, *nephesh ḥayyah*, is the term for whatever lives by breathing—humans, animals and birds. Divine in-breathing, is however, not mentioned for the beasts and birds of 2:19 equally molded out of the ground. Does the specific mention of in-breathing in relation to humans indicate that they are of a higher order? In myths of the neighboring nations, human beings were a composite of earth and the blood of a divine being. Similarly, there is here an earthy and a divine element. This breath of God is, however, not the soul, for ancient Hebrew anthropology did not know the distinction between a material body and a spiritual soul.

14. "And Phison, which denotes a multitude, running into India, makes its exit into the sea, and is by the Greeks called Ganges." *Ant* I.1.3.

15. LXX, followed by Vulgate, has "spring" here.

16. Miller, *Genesis 1–11*, 38.

> ## PSALM 139
>
> Lord, you have probed me, you know me: you know when I sit and stand; you understand my thoughts from afar . . .
> You formed my inmost being; you knit me in my mother's womb. I praise you because I am wonderfully made; wonderful are your works! My very self you know. My bones are not hidden from you; when I was being made in secret, fashioned in the depths of the earth. Your eyes saw me unformed; in your book all are written down; my days were shaped, before one came to be . . . (vv. 1–2, 13–16)

Eden is east of the narrator; there the LORD God planted a garden (2:8),[17] and placed there the man whom he formed. Then, out of the ground, the LORD God made grow every tree delightful to look at and good for food. The viewpoint is that of the man; the narrator will later (3:6) recall these two qualities of the trees of the garden. The Lord God appears here as beneficent and gracious: "the garden is an act of utter graciousness."[18] Genesis 2:15, in a resumptive repetition after the insertion of Gen 2:10–14, refers a second time to the LORD God settling the man in the garden. This time a reason is given: to till it and keep it (NRSV). The man is to take care of the garden for the LORD God. In *Enuma Elish* humans were created to take over the toil of the lesser gods, tilling the field of the gods and celebrating their festivals.

The verb for "settled" is *nuah*, usual for God's giving Israel rest in the promised land, a rest prefaced on obeying God's law (Deut 30:16). Garden is masculine, but "it" is feminine in most manuscripts. Sailhamer[19] thus translates *le-'obdah ule-shamerah*, to worship and obey (command, *siwwah*, is feminine in Hebrew). *Abad* means to work, till, but also to worship when used in religious contexts; *shamar* means to guard, but also to observe a command.[20] This agrees with *Neof*: "to toil in the Law and to observe its

---

17. LXX: *paradeisos* which meant orchard, (walled) garden, but consistently used for God's garden as distinct from secular ones. For how this became paradise, see Jeremias, "Paradeisos," 765–73, and below, under Tradition.

18. Brueggemann, *Genesis*, 45.

19. Sailhamer, *Pentateuch as Narrative*, 100.

20. Cassuto concurs, and refers to the rabbinic interpretation of *le-'obdah* as denoting the sacrifices (*GenR* 16.5): "the rabbinic interpretation of the word *le-'obdah* is seen to

commandments." However, though a retrospective canonical reading may suggest such nuances, they do not yet arise in semiotic chronology; obedience to God's command has not yet featured.

The same phrase, *la-ʿabod ʾet ha-adamah*, occurs as the man's task after expulsion from Eden (3:23). However, in Eden the LORD God already raised for the man trees good for food. The translation above, to till it and keep it (NRSV) is thus problematic. Preferable is "to cultivate and care for it" (NABRE), or in ecological terms, care for it and conserve it.[21] Habel contrasts humankind's mandate in Gen 1:27–28 with the mission in Gen 2:15. There humankind is to rule (*radah*) and subjugate (*kabash*), here to serve (*'abad*) and preserve (*shamar*). In ecological terms this change of language is important.

In the midst of the garden were the tree of life and the tree of the knowledge of good and bad. I translate *raʿ* neutrally as "bad" to avoid the moral note of "evil" at this stage. The man may eat of the tree of life, but of the other tree the Lord God said, *when you eat from it you shall die.* Death is the binary opposite of life, so the tree of knowledge should be the tree of death. The snake will seize on the binary opposition and suggest that the tree contains not death, but godlike qualities the LORD wanted to keep from humans. The tree of life appears in myth. The *Gilgamesh Epic* speaks of the plant of life whose leaves confer eternal youth, making one young again in old age.[22] Emblematic of the life-giving powers of the tree of life were the trees planted in the courtyards of temples. Metaphorically wisdom is a tree of life to those who grasp her (Prov 3:18 and often in this book only) in that it endows them with divine and lasting life.

The tree of the knowledge of good and bad is unique to Israel,[23] in fact, it appears only here in the Hebrew Bible. Plaut[24] outlines three series of interpretations and respective objections. The *ethical* interpretation understands it as knowing good from evil, moral discrimination; eating of it would make them "choosing" creatures. But if the man had no discrimination of right and wrong, how could he be punished for disobedience? Besides, "the command itself presupposes that Adam already knew

---

be not just a homiletical exposition, but the actual meaning of the text." *From Adam to Noah*, 124.

21. Habel, *Ecological Reading of Genesis 1–11*, 53.

22. *ANET*, 96.

23. Sarna, *Understanding Genesis*, 26. See also Cassuto, *From Adam to Noah*, 111.

24. Plaut, *Torah*, 37–38.

the difference between obedience and disobedience."[25] Dunn thus believes the issue is rather moral autonomy, choosing to know for oneself *independent* of God (italics mine). The *intellectual* interpretation understands the phrase as a merism, knowledge of good and bad as knowledge of everything.[26] True, by eating they became like God/the gods, but did they attain omniscience? Finally, the *sexual* interpretation builds on the Hebrew sense of "knowing" as including sexual experience; eating led to the experience of nakedness as shameful. Infants live in a garden of innocence; when they discover the sexual impulse they must leave this garden forever. Mieke Bal (see "Feminist Readings" below) below accentuates the sexual interpretation. However, that would make Gen 3:22 imply sexuality in deity (perhaps in earlier stages of the text?). But Israel, though sometimes portraying God in human terms, nowhere attributes sexuality to her God. Plaut sees the themes as so interwoven "that the fabric of the text exhibits not one theme but all, and each is discernible depending on the light in which the text is viewed."[27] For a way forward, we note that the central focus was that "the tree was desirable for gaining wisdom" (*le-haśkîl*, 3:6). Is the text saying that the trees presented a choice between immortality and knowledge, the couple choosing knowledge, wisdom?[28] Wisdom, a trait of the gods, makes them like gods, knowing good and bad (see discussion below). The LORD reacts to this likeness in Gen 3:22, placing boundary limits and frustrating any further grasping of a divine prerogative (immortality) by placing a guard on the tree of life. Surprisingly, the knowledge gained was awareness of nakedness and shame. Was the LORD God being ironic in saying "the man has become like one of us, knowing good and bad"?

The LORD God proceeds to remedy a deficiency in his product, for *it is not good for the man to be alone* (2:18). This is benevolence, attention to the needs of the man even before man would express the desire. But it also implies that man's realm was on a different level; community with the LORD God is not connatural. For the debate whether making a helper for the man subordinates the woman to him see below (Feminist Readings). The man, *ha-adam*, is grammatically male; in the cultural context the

25. Dunn, *Theology of Paul the Apostle*, 83.

26. In line with this interpretation, Josephus, *Ant* I.1.3, called it the tree of wisdom, *phronēsis*.

27. Plaut, *Torah*, 38.

28. "God stands opposed to humankind not so much in terms of mortality—after the fashion of both Orientals and Greeks—as in terms of knowledge." Sternberg, *Poetics of Biblical Narrative*, 46.

male also stood for the species—"every man and woman." The anomaly is that *ha-adam* does not and cannot fully represent the species; he needs a helper, obviously in terms of procreation.[29] The patriarchal writer assumed the first human to be male, yet the text says that "male" is meaningless without "female."[30] Roles in procreation speak of mutuality; to survive, the human species (*ha-adam*) needs male and female. Beyond this is the need for community written into the human DNA. "I am because we are, and because we are, I am" says an African proverb. The *Compendium of the Social Doctrine of the Church* expressed this need for solidarity in respect of man and woman.

> Woman is the complement of man, as man is the complement of woman: man and woman complete each other mutually, not only from a physical and psychological point of view, but also ontologically . . . "The woman is a 'helper' for the man, just as the man is a 'helper' for the woman!": in the encounter of man and woman a unitary conception of the human person is brought about, based not on the logic of self-centeredness and self-affirmation, but on that of love and solidarity. (no. 147)

The LORD God again formed (using the same verb, *yaṣar* / to mold) from the ground all the beasts and birds. *Ha-adam* gave names to them all. Some affirm this as exercise of dominion; however, the focus is on the phrase "helper suited to him" that frames vv. 18–20. Although the animals were of the same stuff of earth, the man found no community with them; they were of a different realm. The divine solution was to cast a deep sleep on the man and to build up one of his ribs into a woman (*ishshah*). The word for ribs (*ṣal'ōtau*) can also mean side. An ancient Jewish interpretation saw the first man as having two faces or male and female bodies joined together, the LORD God merely splitting them.[31] But, the narrator did not say split. The LORD God *built up* what he took into a woman, hence a fresh creation. When the LORD God brought her to the man, the man said in ecstasy, "This one, this time, is bone of my bones, flesh of my flesh." Rabbi Abin (around 300 CE) observed, "Happy the citizen for whom the king is best man!"[32] The LORD God was Adam's best man; God himself founded the institution of marriage. The expression, bone of my bones, denotes kin-

---

29. Bird, "Genesis I–III," 38.

30. Jobling, "Myth and Its Limits," 41.

31. Rabbi Jeremiah b. Leazar (second half of third century CE) in *GenR* 8.1.

32. *GenR* 18.3.

ship relationship—the woman is "my realm of being." Her name puns on man: *wo*man because taken from man (*ishshah* because from *ish*). In this one case, the man has a birthing role. In a comment, the narrator explains the origin of marriage in the urge that makes a man cleave to his wife (2:24). In Gen 1:28 God endowed male and female with the blessing of progeny; here the focus is on the mutual attraction and bond of man and wife. Both aspects, children and mutual bonding, are equally constitutive of marriage. The text does not suggest early matrilocal marriage, it makes primary the man-wife bond over that of parent-child. The editor remarks that the man and woman were both naked, yet felt no shame (2:25), pointing forward to 3:7.

Expulsion from the Garden, Genesis 3

The man and his wife were both *'arummim* (naked), the snake[33] was *'arūm* more than other wild animals. *'Arūm* can mean wise, but also clever, crafty. The narrator keeps us in suspense about whether this is a positive or negative quality of the snake. Wisdom/craftiness is juxtaposed to nakedness: when the couple gain wisdom/insight, they know themselves to be naked.

The snake was a pervasive and multivalent symbol in the ancient Near East. It symbolized immortality and eternal life, but also fertility and the power of sexuality. In the Gilgamesh Epic, the snake seized the plant of life secured by Gilgamesh and so has power to shed its skin and regain its youth, what is offered here by the tree of life![34] It appeared in cults and images, on the heads of the pharaohs, with Hermes on Aesclepius' staff, on the walls of Assyrian and Babylonian kings.[35] The *caduceus*, emblem of the medical profession, has the snake as symbol of healing. John Skinner[36] notes that "in the sphere of religion the serpent was usually worshiped as a good demon." For the narrator, though, the snake is just one of the wild beasts the LORD God created,[37] albeit a talking one and perhaps standing on legs. The snake

---

33. I follow NABRE in speaking of the snake, not the serpent, which has taken on other connotations. We are dealing with an animal, though one that speaks.

34. Charlesworth, *Good and Evil Serpent*, 295.

35. Ibid., 269, 272.

36. Skinner, *Critical and Exegetical Commentary*, 71–72.

37. Charlesworth, *Good and Evil Serpent*, 298. Charlesworth cites MacCulloch, *Encyclopedia of Religion and Ethics*, 11:403, as opining that the serpent was likely a divine being with superior knowledge and with the desire to help man to the knowledge denied

has not yet become the devil of Wisd 2:23–24 who acted out of envy or the ancient serpent who is called the Devil and Satan of Rev 12:9.

The snake inverted the LORD God's words. The LORD God: *mi-kol 'eṣ ha-gan* (from every tree of the garden) you may eat. The snake: did God say, "*mi-kol 'eṣ ha-gan* (from every tree of the garden) you may *not* eat? "You" is plural, thus includes the man and the woman. The woman replied, *we may eat of the fruit of the trees in the garden* except for the tree in the middle of the garden, of which God said, *you shall not eat it or even touch it lest you die*. In the midst of the garden were two trees, not one (2:9). Did the story originally have one tree in the middle of the garden? In Gen 2:17 God forbade *ha-adam* the tree of the knowledge of good and bad; the woman was not yet there, but somehow came to know of the prohibition. "Lest you die" softens the LORD God's categorical "in the day [*be-yōm*] that you eat of it dying you [singular] will die," that is, you certainly will die. God said nothing about touching the tree. Is the woman building a fence around the command to protect it, or manifesting slight irritation at the command?

HAGGADAH

R. Levi said: imagine a woman borrowing vinegar, who went in to the wife of a snake-charmer and asked her, "how does your husband treat you?" "He treats me with every kindness," she replied, "save that he does not permit me to approach this cask which is full of serpents and scorpions." "It contains all his finery," said the other; he wishes to marry another woman and give it to her." What did she do? She inserted her hand into it, and they began biting her. When her husband came he heard her crying out [with pain]. "Have you touched that cask?" he demanded. Similarly, "hast thou eaten of the tree, whereof I commanded thee . . . ?"
GenR 19.10. R. Levi (290—320 CE)

In the dialogue between snake and woman (Gen 3:1–5), the name of God is consistently Elohim, never YHWH Elohim; the narrator does not allow the snake to pronounce the name YHWH. The narrator makes the snake again directly negate God's very words. God: "in the day/*be-yōm* . . . dying, you will die." Snake: "in the day/*be-yōm* . . . dying, you will *not* die." In fact, *Elohim knows that your eyes will be opened and you will be like Elohim knowing good and bad*. Elohim first takes the singular verb, but then

---

him by the other divinities.

the plural when referring to the couple—a subtle verbal play. The translation, *you shall be like the gods* (NABRE) is to be preferred to "you shall be
like God" (NRSV). It is also possible to translate: "the celestial beings well
know that the moment you eat of it your eyes will be opened and you will
be the same as the celestial beings in knowing good from bad."[38] The snake
claims to know the true mind of God and that God is jealously guarding his
prerogatives. The woman "saw," that is, entering into the snake's way of seeing things,[39] she perceived the tree differently. The eyes-heart correlation
in Hebrew psychology comes into play: "The eyes-heart area of human ca-
pability refers to emotion-fused thinking and its outcome, emotion-fused
thought."[40] The eyes manifest the inner emotions of the heart, the gazing of
the eyes induces and increases the desire of the heart. Hence the admoni-
tion of spiritual masters to "guard the eyes," that is, to control the first urges
of desire by turning away the eyes. The woman, however, continued to gaze
with her mind's eye. We are drawn into her stream of consciousness. The
tree is good to eat—we know this already from 2:9. It is pleasing to the
eyes, literally "desire (*ta'awah*) it is to the eyes." This restates 2:9, *nehmad
le-mar'eh* (delightful to look at), stressing the element of desire. Finally,
we arrive at the focus: to be coveted (*nehmad*) to make one wise (NABRE:
desirable for gaining wisdom). The verbal root here, *śkl*, means to be pru-
dent, have understanding or insight. Insight into the true nature of things,
insight into the true aims of God! "To make one wise" is the counterpart of
the snake's "you will be like Elohim," that is, wisdom as the coveted divine
quality. Wise as God, one can establish one's own reality, one's own good
independent of God! The intentions of God become suspect, trust in God
suffers. She prefers the "good" as she sees it to the good purposed by God.
Sin is never the quest of evil as evil, but of evil under an aspect of good, in
the instant some good or profit to the sinner overwhelms every other good.

Some interpreters do not see her action as flowing from mature delib-
eration and choice. Cassuto[41] is among those who think that the man and
woman were like small children not aware of things around them. The tree
would give them knowledge of the world, and with it care and pain, for in
much wisdom is much vexation (Qoh 1:8). In fact, already in the second

38. Charlesworth, *Good and Evil Serpent*, 299.
39. Cf. Humphreys, *Character of God*, 47.
40. Pilch and Malina, *Biblical Social Values and their Meaning*, 63–64.
41. *From Adam to Noah*, 112.

century CE, Irenaeus of Lyons (125–202 CE) posited that the first couple were like infants in the garden.

> For he was a child and had need to grow so as to come to his full perfection . . . but the man was a little one and his discretion still undeveloped, wherefore he was easily misled by the deceiver . . . Adam and Eve (for this is the name of the woman) were naked and were not ashamed, for their thoughts were innocent and childlike and they had no conception or imagination of the sort that is engendered in the soul by evil through concupiscence, and by lust.[42]

She took some of its fruit and ate it and gave also to her man with her (*'immah*) who ate. *'Immah* does not have to mean the man was with her there and then; it simply postulates companionship. Many interpret this text as the woman "tempting" the man. Bird however points out that the author may have in mind the customary male and female roles in food production and consumption (see discussion later).[43] Westermann[44] notes she may have wanted him to join her in the increase of possibilities. Anyway, the man simply conformed, showing that "mutual support in community can also be mutual support in sin." The snake: *your eyes will be opened* [using root, *pḥq*] . . . *like Elohim knowing* [root *yadaʿ*] *good and bad.* Narrator's report: *the eyes of both were opened* [same root *pḥq*] . . . *they knew* [same root *yadaʿ*] *they were naked.* No wonder Blenkinsopp calls the tree of knowledge, "tree of ambiguous wisdom."[45] The knowledge gained was not ascription to divine status, but shame; shame is born of the consciousness of something not quite right with oneself.[46] Awareness of nakedness implies transition from a preconscious state to new consciousness. In the Atrahasis Epic,[47] Enkidu, half man, half beast, received sexual initiation from a harlot called Siduri. Thereafter the beasts fled from him. Shamhat told him, "As I look at thee, Enkidu, thou art become like a god . . . she pulled off (her) clothing; with one (piece) she clothed him . . . anointed himself with oil, became human." Other translations have, "now you are wise, Enkidu, now you have become like us."[48] Clothing marked Enkidu's transition from animal

---

42. Irenaeus, *Proof of the Apostolic Preaching*, 12, 14.
43. Bird, "Genesis 1–3," 41–42.
44. Westermann, *Genesis 1–11*, 250.
45. Blenkinsopp, *Creation, Uncreation, Recreation*, 57.
46. Cf. Cassuto, *From Adam to Noah*, 137.
47. *ANET*, 77.
48. Matthews and Benjamin, *Old Testament Parallels*, 21.

to human. Westermann believes that the text traces the development of culture—from nakedness to clothing with foliage to clothing with skins.[49]

Hearing the LORD God walking in the cool of the day, the couple hid among the trees. Guilt enters the world and causes them to hide from the LORD God. One may confront one's guilt and seek to come right, or hide and dissimulate it. But how can one hide from the Lord? "If I say, 'surely darkness shall hide me, and night shall be my light!'—darkness is not dark for you and night shines as the day. Darkness and light are but one" (Ps 139:11–12). *Where are you?* This is the Lord refusing to be shut out of their guilty lives and giving them the opportunity to begin the turning back to him—repentance. Goldingay remarks that asking questions to discover things about another person through their answers is a central feature of person-to-person relationship.[50] *I was afraid because I was naked.* Nakedness led to shame and the urge to cover up. Fear implies accountability and reckoning. They have run afoul of the LORD God and could expect consequences. They clearly did not attain the status of divinity. *Who told you that you were naked? Have you eaten from the tree . . . ?* The LORD God knew all along what the effect of eating would be. So why the threat of death? Or, did the LORD God dial back the threat, deciding to relate to humans according to their own decisions? Adam would live 930 years (Gen 5:5). *The woman whom you put here with me.* No longer is she "flesh of my flesh," but now an imposition *you* gave *ʿimmadi* (to be with me), using the same preposition as *ʿimmah* in 3:6. The man blames both the LORD God and the woman. Vital relationships begin to sour. The woman blamed the snake, the man blamed the woman, none takes responsibility.

The assize applies measure for measure. The snake availed of its height and speech to deceive the woman. Height and speech are taken from him, it will crawl on its belly. The snake instigated unlawful eating. It will in turn eat only dust. And not even in the renewal of things in the New Jerusalem will this curse be lifted (Isa 65:25)! The snake made a show of friendliness to hook in the woman. The Lord God put enmity between it and the woman, between its offspring and hers. This explains the mutual fear and conflict between snakes and humans. At Gen 2:19 the snake may have been one of the wild beasts Elohim thought would make a good companion for the man; its good relations with the woman stand reversed. Friendly relationships that lead to sin and transgression often turn into deadly enmities.

49. *Genesis 1–11*, 250.
50. Goldingay, *Israel's Gospel*, 136.

He (collective) *yeshuphka* head, and you *teshuphennū* heel. The same root, *shūph*, is used in both parts of the sentence to portray ongoing warfare between the two species. "He will crush your head, and you will strike his heel" (NIV) is tendentious, for "crush" already points to the definitive victory of the Savior; also "he/his" misses the collective sense of humankind. Better is perhaps, *they will strike at your head, while you strike at their heel* (NABRE). Eventually, even before the Christian era, the snake was identified with the devil, opening the way to a spiritual interpretation that makes Gen 3:15 the first promise of redemption, the Protoevangelium (see later).

A brief look at the snake as a character in this narrative. Some dismiss the snake as just a stand-in for the experience of temptation, as a force that comes upon us as if from outside, the "externality of desire."[51] But, the snake is presented as an agent, an actant, a real character, even if an ambiguous one. The narrator's qualification of it as *'arūm* can mean cunning/crafty or wise. The narrator does not disclose the snake's motivation, whether opposition to God, enabling of humans, or envy of humankind. Later traditions will seize on one or another aspect. The snake was right in one thing: they did not die as threatened. Was the snake also right about God's intentions? At 3:22 the LORD God took action to guard the prerogative of immortality. At 6:3 YHWH frustrated another attempt to live forever by decreeing a span of 120 years. The aspiration of humans to godlikeness is here treated as hubris. On the contrary, Elohim of Genesis 1:26 willed to "make human beings in our image, after our likeness." Is this correction by juxtaposition?

David Penchansky suggests that the LORD God placed the trees right in the middle of the garden, "for the express purpose of providing the first humans a test of their obedience to divine commands . . . the importance of the trees lay . . . in their having been chosen as a site of testing. Through the test Yhwh/Elohim would discover the extent of human loyalty."[52] This is not unlike the command to Abraham in Genesis 22 to offer up Isaac as a holocaust, a story the narrator prefaces with "God put Abraham to the test" (Gen 22:1). God did not carry through the threat of instant death, the first of many times God adapts to the outcome of his relationship with humans.

---

51. Ricoeur, *Symbolism of Evil*, 258–59. Similarly, Cassuto, *From Adam to Noah*, 142, writes that the dialogue actually represents what took place in the woman's mind, between her willingness and her innocence.

52. Penchansky, *What Rough Beast?*, 6. Goldingay suggest as follows: "If they pass the test, as Abraham will, then it can be terminated and they can be given the insight the tree conveys. But they cannot take it. They have to be willing to let God give it" (*Israel's Gospel*, 132).

Some posit that the threat is fulfilled in their becoming mortal or in metaphorical death, that is, the ensuing alienation and estrangement.[53] Be that as it may, it is insightful to interpret the clash between God's threat and its non-fulfillment in the narrative as prodding the reader to search deeper into what might be meant or not by "death" as consequence of disobedience to God.

One word, *iṣabōn* (pain, toil), is common in the punishment of the man and the woman, and it affects them in their specific roles. The woman is wife and mother. As mother, childbearing becomes very painful. As wife, desire for the husband subjects her to his rule; female sexuality is subjugated to the control of males. The companion of 2:18 becomes a master! Is this prescription or description according to the cultural mores of the time, and does the LORD God buy into them?

The man is farmer; he will produce food in painful toil (*'iṣabōn*). Before this, abundant food was at hand in the fruits of the garden. Now he must toil for food all his life. The ground is cursed because of him, shares in his punishment as part of his life support. Judgment on him rubs off on the ground. Cursed ground produces thorns and thistles. Is the ground, *ha-adamah*, treated as a subject, or as appendage to the man? Is this just to the earth? Sin has consequences; the judgments present the consequences of the transgression within the historical context of the author—field toil and pain of childbirth as chief sources of pain for man and woman. Bird raises the hermeneutical question of whether these roles should be absolutized.[54] Wife and mother do not exhaust women's roles, even in the Bible. Men too soon branch out into herding, music, city building, administration, and so on.[55] How do we interpret the punishments in reference to these other roles? The man is punished especially because *you listened to your wife and ate*. Does the LORD God uphold patriarchy? Taken from the ground, the man's destiny will be the ground: *for you are dust, and to dust you shall return* (part of the rite of Ash Wednesday). Is this definitive? Belief in afterlife will arise and the tradition will reopen the graves (Dan 12:1–3). The LORD God expels the man from the garden and sets a guard on the tree of life: "expulsion prevents the humans from closing the difference between them

---

53. Moberly, *Theology of the Book of Genesis*, 84–85.

54. "Genesis 1–3," 39n29.

55. Fewell and Gunn, "Shifting the Blame," 36.

and God by eating from the tree of life."[56] For a brief reflection on curse, see Genesis 4.

HEAVEN WITHDRAWS, ORIGIN OF DEATH

Many traditional peoples recount a mythical version of an "Original Sin." In the beginning, heaven was close to earth; a ladder linked the two. God would descend to enjoy the company of human beings, and they could visit God through the ladder. One day, a woman was grinding corn and would continually hit the firmament of heaven with the pestle. In response, God withdrew the heavens on high, humans lost the familiar proximity to God.

They recount the origin of death as follows. It was God's wish that humans should live forever. So God sent the hare and the tortoise with different messages to humankind. The hare runs fast, so God entrusted it with the message, "you, humans, shall be immortal." The tortoise, on the other hand, was entrusted with the message, "you, humans, shall be mortal." The hare ran off, and miles ahead it began to rest and dozed off. The tortoise passed him and reached humankind first. It had just proclaimed, "you, humans, shall be mortal," when the hare ran up with his message. But the harm had been done, and that is why humans are mortal.

The man gave his wife the name Eve. Some interpreters (see Feminist Readings) insist that the character Eve starts here and the name Eve must not be given to the earlier phases of the woman. The narrator explains the name as mother of all the living. Is this a defiant gesture by the man or an act of faith[57] in the future? *Ḥawwah*[58] contains the element, *ḥw*, found also in the name YHWH, and which means "to be" or "cause to be." Does the narrator play with the analogy of *Ḥawwah* as also "creator" of life (cf. 4:1)?

The LORD God made for the man and his wife garments of skin. Now that they need to distinguish themselves from animals, the LORD God himself introduces an element of culture, proper clothing. Although he has just severely censured them, he does not withdraw his care and compassion from them, but continues to stay in relationship. He seems to accept the reality of their new consciousness and assists them in preserving their

---

56. Ibid., 37.

57. Cf. Humphreys, *Character of God*, 52.

58. Cassuto, *From Adam to Noah*, 170–71, recalls Aramaic *ḥiweya'* and Arabic *ḥayyatun*, both meaning serpent; so the man named his wife Female Serpent/Seducer.

dignity.[59] This is the concept of grace, even if the term itself is lacking here. Did the Lord God shed the blood of innocent animals for this purpose? Generally, the Fathers saw the LORD God stripping them of the garments of innocence and immortality[60] (in theological terms called original grace), the garments of skin being a symbol of their new state of mortality, physical and spiritual. Irenaeus believes that Adam showed his repentance in covering himself with fig leaves, when there were many other trees that would irritate his body less.[61]

Behold the man has become like one of us lā-daⓍat ṭōb wa-raⓍ, knowing good and bad. This Hebrew term is fixed; it is always the tree *lā-daⓍat ṭōb wa-raⓍ* (2:9, 17). The LORD God is speaking to the divine council, originally the pantheon, but in Israel beings in YHWH's realm who serve him and carry out his purposes. They resemble the LORD God in being; they share in the knowledge of good and bad. Woman and man aspired to become like one of these. Is the LORD God being ironic here? The step he took belies this reasoning. The man has grasped at a divine quality, so must be prevented from eating of the tree of life and living forever, another divine quality. But this tree was not forbidden; in the garden the man could eat of it, but after his transgression he may not? The LORD God expelled the man from the garden to work the ground from which he was taken. The original placement in the garden was an act of beneficence. Israel could have read this story as a parable of the settlement in, and exile from, the promised land.

The king of Tyre, "full of wisdom [*ḥokmah*], perfect in beauty," was put in Eden, the garden of God (Ezek 28:12, 13). But when wisdom and insight (*tebūnah*) made him pretend to be a god at heart, he received the sentence, "therefore I banished you from the mountain of God" (Ezek 28:2, 16). Equally here, "wisdom" that induces illusions of divinity, is quickly put in check. Although the language of Fall does not occur, the Christian church reads Genesis 3 as the account of "The Fall" (see below). Within the context of Genesis 3–6, one is impressed how one story after another portrays how wrongdoing entered the world to dominate humankind. Choices at the beginning seem to have determined the current human condition:

59. Habel, *Ecological Reading of Genesis 1–11*, 63.

60. For example, Augustine, *On the Trinity*, 12.11.16 (ACCS, 98): "[Adam and Eve], who were stripped of their first garments of [innocence], deserved by their mortality garments of skin."

61. *Against Heresies*, 3.23. 5, in ACCS, 82.

"the first human beings acted in a way that had decisive implications for everyone who would come after."[62] It is this trajectory that the doctrine of original sin and the fall seek to trace.

Cherubim and the revolving sword are placed east of Eden to guard the way to the tree of life. The man was driven further east; in this narrative east is place of banishment, for example, Cain settled in the land of Nod, east of Eden (4:16). On the cherubim, see Cassuto's comparisons with the text of Ezekiel 28 and 31 above. James Barr[63] contends that the story of Genesis 2–3 is a story of how immortality was almost gained but in fact was lost. In Gen 3:22–24, only the man is mentioned. Is this recognition of the man's cultural role as representative of the family?

How does the LORD God come off as a character in this section? What stands out in this unit is immanence: the LORD God is fully involved with the life of the man and the woman. He provides for them, asks questions, reacts to their foibles, but never gives up the relationship. Having threatened death, he ended up clothing the man and his wife. He is in closer life-giving contact with things; he plants a garden, molds a human figure and breathes life into it. He has a second go at creation, remedying aspects of it that have proven "not good"—it is not good for the man to be alone. As solution, he tried the animals and ended with the solution of the creation of woman. The image is that of a God who adapts, who accompanies humans in the ups and downs of life. However, this God also gives commands to be obeyed, with consequences for non-obedience: "rebellion against or disobedience toward God and his laws results in banishment/estrangement and, literally or figuratively, death."[64] He frustrates the striving of humans to make themselves into gods or to grasp at being like God, in contrast to Elohim of Gen 1:26–27 who created humans to be in God's image and likeness. It may be that "expulsion prevents the humans from closing the difference between them and God by eating from the tree of life."[65] It may also be "a natural consequence of knowing good and evil. To know good *and evil* in paradise would hardly be possible."[66] The LORD God simply let humans have what they wanted, which is the choice of discerning their way through the ups and downs of life, and for good measure increasing the

62. Goldingay, *Israel's Gospel*, 144–145.

63. Barr, *Garden of Eden and the Hope of Immortality*.

64. Fox, *Five Books of Moses*, 18.

65. Fewell and Gunn, "Shifting the Blame," 37.

66. Ibid.

pains. St. Ambrose answers those who "seem to accuse [God] of being so devoid of beneficence as to be unwilling to pardon when he had the power to do so or of being powerless if he was unable to forgive."[67] Disobedience was the cause of death, so the cause was man, not God. The reader should note that true forgiveness, as contrasted with reconciliation after punishment, did not enter the narrative till Moses pestered God after the sin of the Golden Calf (Exod 32).

Excursus: Feminist Readings

I briefly summarize some feminist approaches to Genesis 2–3. Feminist biblical interpreters uphold the liberation of women, and that through the text of the Bible—the Bible as both oppressor and liberator of women. Three types of feminist approaches are *radical, neo-orthodox,* and *critical.*[68] Radical feminists believe that the Bible is irremediably androcentric and thus has no authority. The neo-orthodox single out some liberative texts or sections which they use as a "canon within the canon." Critical feminists seek to reconstruct liberative roles for women by recovering elements from the Jesus movement and the ministry of Paul. The literature is vast, so dialogue with a couple of feminists must suffice.

Phyllis Trible[69] lists these eleven principal arguments for misogyny and sets out to refute them:

- A male God creates first man (2:7) and last woman (2:22); first means superior and last means inferior or subordinate.

- Woman is created for the sake of man: a helpmate to cure his loneliness (2:18–23).

- Contrary to nature, woman comes out of man; she is denied even her natural function of birthing and that function is given to man (2:21–22).

- Woman is the rib of man, dependent upon him for life (2:21–22).

- Taken out of man (2:23), woman has a derivative, not an autonomous existence.

- Man names woman (2:23) and thus has power over her.

67. ACCS, 96.
68. See Okoye, *Scripture in the Church,* 66–69.
69. Trible, "A Love Story Gone Awry," 73.

- Man leaves his father's family in order to set up through his wife another patriarchal unit (2:24).

- Woman tempted man to disobey and thus she is responsible for sin in the world (3:6); she is untrustworthy, gullible, and simpleminded.

- Woman is cursed by pain in childbirth (3:16); pain in childbirth is a more severe punishment than man's struggles with the soil; it signifies that woman's sin is greater than man's.

- Woman's desire for man (3:16) is God's way of keeping her faithful and submissive to her husband.

- God gives man the right to rule over woman (3:16).

She insists that *ha-adam* was sexually undifferentiated and should be translated as an "it." *Ha-adam* as masculine is only grammatical gender, not sexual identity; sexual gender enters only at 2:22 when the creation of woman ushers in the bifurcation of *ish/ishshah* (man and wife). Woman as ⊠*ezer* should not be translated "helper" or support, rather "companion" (anyway, ⊠*ezer* in itself comports no inferior status, as God is often called ⊠*ezer*). "She shall be called *ishshah*" is no naming of the woman—this would give the man dominion over her as over the animals—but only recognition of sexual difference. Creation after and from the man implies no inferior status, in fact the man was a rough draft, woman the culmination of creation. Both the man and the woman transgressed equally; she did not "tempt" him. Besides, her motives were aesthetic, his those of the belly. "He will rule over you" (Gen 3:16) is not punishment (lacks the usual protasis, "because you have done this"), rather mere declaration of a consequence of her action.

Mieke Bal[70] sees Genesis 1–2 as one coherent story in which Genesis 1 retrospectively completed the imaginary representation of creation through differentiation in Genesis 2. She argues from the nature of character in narrative and what she calls *retrospective fallacy*, that is, "projection of an accomplished and singular named character onto previous textual elements that lead to the construction of that character."[71] Specifically, she argues that *ha-adam* of Gen 2:7 was a sexless creature, a "clod." Then the one singular creature becomes plural when YHWH God himself decided that his work was unfinished, for it is not good for the man to be alone.

70. Bal, "Sexuality, Sin and Sorrow," 104–30.
71. Ibid., 108.

To say, "a helper fit for him," is faulty translation, for there was as yet no "he," differentiation had not stepped in. A rib taken from the earth creature could be euphemism for belly, hence a womb. Or the reference could be to the element -*ti* in the name of the goddess Nin-ti created from Enki's rib; *ti* means rib, but also "the making of life" (compare "mother of all living, Gen 3:20).[72] Woman appears first and changes the meaning of *ha-adam* from earthbeing to earth man; in that sense, they mutually define each other. "Taken from *ish*/man" (2:23) does not posit the priority of man; the phrase should not be read as "made out of," rather "taken away from," in the sense of differentiated from, man.[73] The tree of knowledge offers knowledge that includes sexual knowledge (*yada'* means to know, but also to have sex). "It does indeed supply immortality, not to the individual but to the species."[74] For, "once sexuality is accepted, humanity can do without impossible immortality."[75] Sexual knowledge makes you die and not die, you live on in the children. The wisdom alluded to cannot but be the acceptance of the human condition, including death, and the continuity of history that it allows. What was at issue was capacity for differentiation. Both the LORD God and the serpent withhold information but are not lying. The LORD God stresses one aspect, mortality, the serpent the other, knowledge. Both trick humans into accepting the unavoidable, that is, into renouncing the childish fantasy of individual immortality.[76] The LORD God's recognition of the couple's divine likeness (3:22) is ironic reversal of what he really thinks; how else account for his fear and defensiveness? The woman's disobedience is the first independent act, which makes her powerful as a character. "She has the power to make the man eat, make him know (her), and disobey in his turn, also to turn the almighty God in Genesis 1 into a character with equal status, equal features and feelings to the others."[77] She realizes the creation of humanity in God's likeness and of God in human likeness. The free will to act put a stop to God's exclusive power of Genesis 1; the relationship becomes horizontal. Performative speech becomes dialogue, shared power installs confrontation and struggle.[78] The woman did

72. Ibid., 115.
73. Ibid., 117.
74. Ibid., 122.
75. Ibid.
76. Ibid., 123.
77. Ibid., 125.
78. Ibid.

not exactly sin, she opted for reality. Rather than punishment, the LORD God's reaction to the couple should be taken as "an explicit spelling out of the consequences of the human option."[79] Is it possible that the words to Cain, "and unto you shall be his desire and you shall rule over him" (Gen 4:7), was originally part of the LORD God's speech to the woman, thus subordinating the man to her? Anyway, God fixes sexual roles here—fertility and domination: "fertility necessitates labor, and domination presupposes desire as its precondition."[80] Dominators are as insecure as the dominated. The story set out to communicate male priority and superiority and justify the social dominance of men over women, but texts often say more than, and sometimes even quite the opposite of, what they intend. As creator/provider of "all living," Eve, *ḥawwah*, as a name resembles that of YHWH; both share the element, *ḥw* (to be, cause to be).[81]

Meyers translates 3:16 as follows: "I will greatly increase your toil and your pregnancies, (along) with travail shall you beget children, for to your man is your desire and he shall predominate over you."[82] Increased productivity and procreativity are mandated. *Iṣābōn* has the same meaning in 3:16 and 3:17, namely, physical labor, precisely of agricultural work in an unfriendly environment. "He shall rule over you" is no general assertion of male dominance, rather restricted within the context of the woman's sexual desire. Mortal risks attached to childbearing. Yet, motherhood is in the national interest, so the male's will in the area of sexuality is imposed on her. But such male control is not experienced as oppressive, because of the natural yearning for him.

Susan Lanser responds to Trible and Bal with incisive critiques.[83] Hearers in the ancient cultural context would not ordinarily hear the *ha-adam* of 2:7 as sex-neutral. She points out that "she shall be called *ishshah* because she was taken from *ish*" would be meaningless if there were no *ish* prior to this. And if *ha-adam* became a new being, *ha-ish*, why does the text continue to use *ha-adam*? That the LORD God set out to make a helper fit for *ha-adam* points to the centrality of *ha-adam*. The man is punished, among other things, for listening to the voice of his wife (Gen 3:12). How explain the fact that male dominance ("he shall rule over you," 3:16) enters

79. Ibid.
80. Ibid., 127.
81. Ibid., 129.
82. Meyers, *Discovering Eve*, 95–121.
83. Lanser, "Feminist Criticism in the Garden," 67–84.

for a crime of which man and woman are equally responsible if it were not that the woman was assumed more guilty and in need of guidance? The important question may be one of location, from whose grammatical principles and cultural attitudes one is reading. Reading sequentially, tension appears between the theologically egalitarian impulse in Genesis 1 and the seemingly patriarchal Genesis 2–3 that reflects the status of woman in traditional Israelite society. This might signify some ambivalence about the place of woman, a patriarchy beginning to be uncomfortable with itself.

Bird points specifically to the "image of God" as defining man and woman in Genesis 1.[84] The writer of that chapter associates image with the male experience of ruling and governing. Ongoing reflection need draw out the content of "image" from the experience of the species as a whole, including female models of relationship, rather than solely male models of dominion and subjugation. Rather than Trible's contrast of woman's reflective act and man's belly-oriented acquiescence, the author may have in mind the customary male and female roles in food production and consumption.[85]

Tradition

Paradise. The garden of Eden soon became Paradise, the place of the righteous. The LXX had consistently used the word *paradeisos*, which meant orchard or walled garden, for God's garden as distinct from secular ones. The garden contained the tree of life which would make people live forever. When faith in eternal life arose, the tree of life became the portion of the righteous. If cherubim and the flaming sword guarded the way to the tree, it was only to reserve it for the righteous. Paradise came to mean the place of final reward for the righteous.[86] Recounting Enoch's journeys, the Book of Watchers, late third century BCE, says:

> I passed by the paradise of righteousness, and I saw from afar trees more plentiful and larger than these trees . . . and the tree of wisdom, whose fruit the holy ones eat and learn great wisdom . . . and its fragrance penetrates far beyond the tree.[87]

84. Bird, "Genesis 1–3," 41, 42.

85. Ibid., 37n22.

86. Kugel, *Bible as It Was*, 79.

87. Nickelsburg and VanderKam, *I Enoch*, 47–48.

Notice how attention veers from the tree of life to focus uniquely on the tree of the knowledge of good and bad, called simply the tree of wisdom. In this book, *the* human quest is that of wisdom. It was only natural that soon paradise would become a place in heaven. Jesus said to the Good Thief: "Today you will be with me in Paradise" (Luke 23:43). Paul was "caught up to the third heaven . . . into Paradise and heard ineffable things, which no one may utter" (2 Cor 12:2–3).

Marriage. The text takes monogamy for granted, also that marriage is between man and woman; recent arguments about same-sex marriage seek support in other texts. Lamech was the first to take two wives (Gen 4:19). In the Old Testament period, polygamy was practiced. Jacob, ancestor of Israel, married two sisters, each of whom also gave him her maid (Gen 29–30). Solomon had as wives seven hundred princesses and three hundred concubines (2 Kgs 11:3); what was condemned was only that they were foreign women who enticed him into false worship. It may be that remembrance of this lead Deut 17:17 to prescribe for the king, "neither shall he have a great number of wives, lest his heart turn away." There was even an obligation of levirate marriage, whereby one must marry a brother's widow if he dies without a son (Deut 25:5), a custom the Sadducees used to confront Jesus about the resurrection life (Mark 12:18–27). For various reasons, partly cultural and economic, monogamy seems to have become the general practice by the time of Jesus.

EPHESIANS 5:23–33

Husbands, love your wives, even as Christ loved the church and handed himself over for her to sanctify her, cleansing her by the bath of water with the word, that he might present to himself the church in splendor, without spot or wrinkle or any such thing, that she might be holy and without blemish. So also husbands should love their wives as their own bodies. He who loves his wife loves himself . . . "For this reason a man shall leave father and mother and be joined to his wife, and the two shall become one flesh." This is a great mystery, but I speak in reference to Christ and the church (Eph 5:23–33).

The right of a man to divorce his wife "because he finds in her something indecent" (Deut 24:1–4) was still upheld; but woman had no right to divorce the husband. The Pharisees asked Jesus about this law. Jesus' reply is in its most radical in Mark. Citing both Gen 1:27 and 2:23, Jesus declared that neither may divorce the other, on pain of adultery. The highest thing to be said about marriage is that the bond between the Christian husband and wife symbolizes that between Christ and his church (see text box on Eph 5:25–33).

The Serpent Becomes the Devil and Satan.[88] Satan appeared in Job 1–2 to test Job's piety, but as one of the sons of God. The Hebrew word *śaṭan* means adversary, assayer; devil comes from Greek *diabolos*, meaning slanderer. In Zech 3:1–2, Satan stood at the right of the high priest Joshua to accuse him before God. In 2 Sam 24:1, YHWH incited David to take a census of the people, but 1 Chr 21:1 displaced this to Satan, who was beginning to take on negative features. Tradition soon arose of heavenly beings falling from heaven and corrupting humanity. Isaiah 14:12 symbolized the king of Babylon as the Morning Star, son of the Dawn, fallen down from heaven to earth. *1 Enoch* 6–11 (late third century BCE) presented a rebellion in heaven and the fall to earth of the watchers, sons of heaven, under the leadership of Shemihazah; they took wives of the daughters of men and taught humankind all iniquity. *1 En* 69:6 accuses Gadre'el as being the one who led Eve astray. The context was ripe to interpret the snake of *I will put enmity between you and the woman, and between your offspring and hers* as an evil serpent, devil, or Satan. So Wisd 2:24, "by the envy of the devil, death entered the world." Rev 12:9 speaks of "the huge dragon, the ancient serpent who is called the Devil and Satan who deceived the whole world." And the devil (Matt 4; Luke 4) or Satan (Mark 1:13) tempted even Jesus.

The Evil Inclination (yetzer ha-ra'). Judaism entertains no doctrine of original sin. Only death came with Adam's sin, not the necessity to sin: "you laid upon him one commandment of yours; but he transgressed it, and immediately you appointed death for him and for his descendants" (4 Ezra 3:7). Urbach asserts that no Tanna[89] among the disciples of Akiba (martyred 132 CE) attributed the existence of sin to Adam's transgression.[90] Kugel asserts, though, that the idea of hereditary sin occurs in Jewish texts of the first century CE.[91] For example, in the *Life of Adam and Eve*[92] Adam says to Eve, "What have you done? You have brought upon us a great

88. Kugel, *Bible as It Was*, 72–74.

89. Tanna derives from Aramaic "to teach" and is a name given to Jewish rabbis mentioned in the Mishnah (200 CE) and the Baraita.

90. Urbach, *Sages*, 426.

91. Kugel, *Bible as It Was*, 72.

92. Latin text around 400 CE, original Hebrew between 100 BCE and 200 CE.

wound, transgression and sin in all our generations."[93] Ben Sira 25:24[94] says, "With a woman sin had a beginning, and because of her we all die."[95] 4 Ezra 3:21–23 (ca. 100 CE) clearly traces sin from Adam: "For the first Adam, burdened with an evil heart, transgressed and was overcome, as were also all who were descended from him. Thus the disease became permanent." The author later cried, "O Adam, what have you done? For though it was you who sinned, the fall was not yours alone, but ours also who are your descendants" (7:118).[96] However, the contemporary 2 Bar 54:15, 19 counters that each one born of Adam "has prepared for himself the coming torment. And further, each of them has chosen for himself the coming glory . . . Adam is, therefore, not the cause, except only for himself, but each of us has become our own Adam."[97] Later Jews largely abandoned the idea of inherited sin when Christians championed it. There was always a current that asserted that humans could keep God's law, for example, Ben Sira 15:14, "God in the beginning created human beings and made them subject to their own free choice. If you choose, you can keep the commandments." For "free choice," the Hebrew text (Cairo Geniza) has *yeṣer*. Jewish theology speaks of the *yeṣer ha-ṭōv* (the good inclination) and *yeṣer ha-ra*⊠[98] (the evil inclination, evil desire, evil impulse), terms probably coined from Gen 6:5, *every desire [yēṣer] that their heart conceived was always nothing but evil*, and 8:21, *since the desires of the human heart are evil from youth*. God created both inclinations in humans. The "evil inclination" can lead to sin, but is neither sinful nor implies a state of sin. When in a discussion on Job, Raba (ca. 350 CE) seemed to exculpate evil by saying God created both virtuous people and wicked people, his companions shot him down saying, "if God created the evil inclination, he also created the Torah as its antidote."[99] In fact, Rabbi Na⊠man (died 320 CE) insists that when it is said

93. Charlesworth, *Old Testament Pseudepigrapha*, 276.

94. Hebrew original about 186 BCE.

95. From the context of the discussion of bad wives, Porter, "Pauline Concept of Original Sin," 17, vainly argues that this means "a wife is the origin of sin, and it is through her that we husbands all die."

96. Text from Charlesworth, *Old Testament Pseudepigrapha*, 529 and 541, respectively.

97. Ibid., 640.

98. The earliest attestation of the full term, *yeṣer ha-ra'* [ayin], seems to be in the Qumran "Plea for Deliverance," 11QPsa 19:15, dated first half of the first century CE, in which the psalmist prays that the evil impulse may not take possession of his limbs. See Otzen, *TDOT*, 6:265.

99. b. Baba Bathra 16a, cited from http://www.come-and-hear.com/bababathra/

that God saw all he created and it was "very good," this included the evil inclination: "but for the evil desire, however, no man would build a house, take a wife and beget children."[100]

The Fall. No terms designating a fall appear in Genesis 2–3. However, sequential reading from Genesis 1 (all creation "very good," Gen 1:31) gives the impression of a slide from good to evil. In Isa 14:12, the king of Babylon hears the elegy, "how you have fallen from the heavens, O Morning Star, son of the Dawn." The Latin Vulgate rendered this: "*quomodo cecidisti de caelo Lucifer.*" Lucifer, light-bearer, is epithet of Venus, the Morning Star; this word has been transferred to Satan. The Hebrew renders "you have fallen" with *naphalta*, the same root, *naphal*, as in the word, Nephilim (Gen 6:4), the fallen ones, whose myth we read of in *1 En* 7:1–2, that is, angelic beings who descended on earth to corrupt people in various ways. Elsewhere we read of the "fall" of the king of Tyre banished from Eden, the mountain of God, and driven out by the cherubs (Ezek 28:16–170). Apparently the first explicit use of the language of "the fall" with respect to Adam is extra-biblical: 4 Ezra 7:118 reads, "O Adam, what have you done? For though it was you who sinned, the fall was not yours alone, but ours also who are your descendants." In the Apocalypse of Moses 20:2[101] Adam reports that "my eyes were opened and I knew that I was naked of the righteousness with which I had been clothed. And I wept saying, 'why have you done this to me, that I have been estranged from my glory with which I was clothed?'" Augustine says that Adam and Eve were stripped of their first garment of innocence.[102] Christianity read this as a fall from original grace and righteousness.

Original Sin, Adam-Christ Typology. Hints of hereditary sin or universal sinfulness can be heard in Gen 6:5 and 8:21 (see above). Other texts include, Ps 51:7, "behold I was born in guilt, in sin my mother conceived me"; Jer 17:1, "the sin of Judah is written with an iron stylus, engraved . . . upon the tablets of their hearts." Paul cites Ps 14:1, 3, "there is no one just, not one, there is no one who understands, there is no one who seeks God. All have gone astray . . . there is no one who does good, not even one," to make his point that all, Jew and Greek, have sinned and are deprived of the

---

bababathra_16.html.

100. *GenR* 9.7.

101. A recension of *The Life of Adam and Eve*, the Hebrew original being between 100 BCE and 200 CE.

102. *On the Trinity*, 12.11.16, in ACCS, 98.

glory of God" (Rom 3:25). He next argues from the Adam-Christ typology, Rom 5:12–21. Adam is head of a sinful people, Christ the head of those justified.[103] Critical is Rom 5:12, "just as through one person sin entered the world, and through sin, death, and thus death came to all *eph' hō* all sinned." Dunn prefers to render the Greek phrase as "for this reason, because," that is, all do sin and so validate for themselves the death of Adam.[104] "Death" is understood as both physical and spiritual, for it requires the act of the redeemer. Irenaeus was the first known Father of the church to use the Adam-Christ typology,[105] applying his doctrine of Christ's recapitulation of the work of creation:

> For it behooved him who was to destroy sin and redeem man under the power of death, that he should himself be made that very same thing which he was, that is, man; who had been drawn by sin into bondage, but was held by death, so that sin should be destroyed by man, and man should go forth from death. (*Against Heresies* III.18.7)[106]

The Vulgate translated the Greek phrase as *in quo*, in whom; that is, when Adam sinned, all his descent also sinned. Is this to say that humankind was constituted sinners as result of Adam? Because he sinned as the legal representative of his race, they are counted guilty of his sin? There would be tension between destiny and individual action.[107] Anyway, Augustine based himself on the Vulgate to elaborate what became the church's doctrine of original sin. He interprets Paul as professing *hereditary* guilt: Adam's sin was *peccatum originans* (originating sin), the impact on his posterity *peccatum originatum* (originated sin):

> Our nature was already present in the seed from which we were to spring. And because this nature has been soiled by sin and doomed to death and justly condemned, no human being was to be born in the human race in any other condition.[108]

---

103. Porter, "Pauline Concept of Original Sin," 26.

104. *Theology of Paul the Apostle*, 95n76.

105. See VanMaaren, "The Adam-Christ Typology," 282.

106. http://www.newadvent.org/fathers/0103318.htm.

107. Porter, "Pauline Concept of Original Sin," 28.

108. *City of God*, 13, 14, cited from Hayes, *Gift of Being*, 92.

> ### CATECHISM #404
> Adam had received original holiness and justice not for himself alone, but for all human nature. By yielding to the tempter, Adam and Eve committed a personal sin, but this sin affected the human nature that they would then transmit in a fallen state. It is a sin which will be transmitted by propagation to all mankind, that is, by the transmission of a human nature deprived of original holiness and justice. And that is why original sin is called "sin" only in an analogical sense: it is a sin "contracted" and not "committed"—a state and not an act (*Catechism of the Catholic Church*, # 404).

The Protoevangelium. Irenaeus of Lyons (125–202 CE) seems to be the first to read Gen 3:15 as the first announcement of the coming salvation, the *Protoevangelium*. He wrote:

> For this end did he put enmity between the serpent and the woman and her seed, they keeping it up mutually; he the sole of whose foot should be bitten, having power also to tread upon the enemy's head; but the other biting, killing, and impeding the steps of man, until the seed did come appointed to tread down his head . . . which was born of Mary, of whom the prophet speaks, "thou shalt tread upon the asp and the basilisk, thou shalt trample down the lion and the dragon" (Ps 91:13).[109]

The Vulgate (not the Septuagint) read, *ipsa conteret caput tuum*, she will crush your head. The church of the West sees this fulfilled in the Virgin Mary, mother of the Redeemer, thus the custom of statues of the Virgin having her feet crushing the head of a snake.

Eve-Church, Eve-Mary Typology. Justin Martyr (120–165 CE) was apparently the first to make the Eve-Mary typology.

> For Eve, being a virgin and undefiled, conceiving the word that was from the serpent, brought forth disobedience and death; but the Virgin Mary, taking faith and joy, when the angel told her the good tidings that the Spirit of the Lord should . . . overshadow her, and therefore the Holy One that was born of her was Son of God, answered, "be it done to me according to thy word."[110]

The Fathers also wove an Eve-Church typology, playing with the use of the same verb, "to build": The Lord God *built* the rib into a woman (Gen

109. *Against Heresies* III.23.7. See also *Against Heresies*, bk. 3, ch. 23, in *Ante-Nicene Fathers*, ed. Alexander et al., http://www.newadvent.org/fathers/0103323.htm.

110. *Dialogue with Trypho*, 305 (ch. 100).

2:22); you are fellow citizens and members of the household of God *built* upon the foundation of the apostles and prophets (Eph 2:19–20).

> Adam's sleep was a mystical foreshadowing of Christ's death, and when his dead body hanging from the cross was pierced by the lance, it was from his side that there issued forth that blood and water that, as we know, signifies the sacraments by which the church is built up. "Built" is the very word the Scripture uses in connection with Eve.[111]

---

111. Augustine, *City of God*, 22.17, in ACCS, 70.

CHAPTER 4

Genesis 4:1–26

Cain and Abel; Origins of Culture and Worship

For three crimes of Edom, and now four—I will not take it back—
Because he pursued his brother with the sword; suppressing all pity,
persisting in his anger, his wrath raging without end.

—Amos 2:11

We consider Genesis 4:1—6:4 a narrative unit, though we divide it into two chapters, the current one and the next. Genesis 4:25–26 is a suture (see below) that links two genealogies, the Cainite and the Sethite, Gen 4:17–24 and 5:1-32. Genesis 6:1-4 has no grammatical links with the story of the flood. Contrary to some who read it as the immediate cause of the flood, or the hundred and twenty years as respite period before the flood, I read it as another example in a pattern of transgressions in Genesis 1-11, each calling forth the divine response.

The "gaps" in this narrative section are many; translators and scholars seek to close them in various ways. Giving birth to Cain, Eve said, "*I have produced a male child with the help of the LORD*"(4:1). But the verb *qanītī* means "to create" or "to possess" (see Prov 8:22), and the Hebrew word *'ish* does not mean "a male child," rather a grown-up man. The sign of the accusative in ⊠*et-yhwh* seems to portray the *'ish* as the LORD. In fact, some midrash texts speak of Cain as seed of Eve and one of the (evil) divine beings.[1] Translators take the preposition here to mean "with (the help of) YHWH,"

---

1. *Ps-Jonathan* at Gen 4:1: Adam knew that his wife had conceived by Sammael, the angel of the Lord.

a meaning now attested in a cognate language.² A meaning, "from," has also been attested in Akkadian, *šamū ʿitti* (to buy from).³ How could Abel be a shepherd and kill animals for his offering when Adam/humankind was assigned the tilling of the ground and killing meat was not permitted till Gen 9:3–4 (to Noah)? In v. 7, the Lord said, *if you act rightly, you will be accepted.* Literally, the second part has just one word, *śĕ☒t*, which means "lifting up" (see below for efforts to close this gap). Verse 8a has only *Cain said to his brother Abel*, with the verb, *☒amar*, which requires a complement, unlike *dibber*, to speak, which does not. The story continues with, *when they were in the field, Cain attacked his brother Abel and killed him.* The Septuagint, inferring from what follows, supplied a complement, "let us go out into the plain," and other versions followed suit. The distinction between settlement area and field area presumes developments that came later. Cain's saying, *anyone may kill me at sight* (v. 14) and the text, *Cain knew his wife* (v. 17a), both suggest an original setting in an already developed population, for where else could he get a wife and who else would kill him? How did Cain, cursed to be a perpetual vagrant, found a city (v. 17)? For whom is this city? Or is this a different Cain? The cursed Cain became father of a whole line, including Lamech. Is this same as the Lamech who begot Noah (Gen 5:30), the ancestor of humankind? Cain apparently did not transmit his curse, for Cainites began to settle in cities. In the days of Enosh, *people began to invoke the LORD by name* (4:26). Wasn't the LORD already known in the garden and "invoked" by Eve in 4:1? These issues will be discussed as we proceed.

After the transgression of the first couple, we meet here yet another wrongdoing—the killing of a brother by a brother. Soon we hear Lamech's "Song of the Sword" (Gen 4:23–24) and read of the sons of God taking the daughters of humans as wives (Gen 6:1–4).⁴ Unlike creation myths that glorify the beginnings, the biblical writer paints a dark picture of human

2. Cf. Blenkinsopp, *Creation, Un-creation, Recreation,* 84, note 3, refers to a parallel in Atrahasis where the mother-goddess Mami proposes to create humans *itti Enkima,* "with (the help of) Enki."

3. Hamilton, *Book of Genesis,* 221.

4. Goldingay, *Israel's Gospel,* 144, correctly notes that "Genesis 1–3 only begins the narrative portrayal of the origins of human wrongdoing. It is Genesis 1–6 or Genesis 1–11 as a whole that offers the total portrait." Westermann, *Genesis 1–11,* 304, 318–19, wonders whether one could speak of intensification of sin and answers that this is not quite accurate. "Intensification" would seem to say that what was really decisive took place with the fall (generally restricted to the area of sex), ignoring the social aspect of the proclamation.

origins, creating a pattern that insinuates that something went wrong in the human condition right from the beginning (see the last chapter on the fall and original sin).

Cain and Abel, Gen 4:1–16

The narrative focus is on Cain, Abel is mostly qualified as "his brother." In this narrative, "brother" occurs seven times, as if to highlight the enormity of the crime—fratricide. *Hebel* in Hebrew denotes vapor, mist, vanity—what is ephemeral, not lasting, what is of short duration. Some scholars think that the name Abel was derived from the narrative itself. Abel branched into the keeping of flocks, even though Adam had been condemned to "till the ground from which he had been taken" (Gen 3:23). Cain continued Adam's vocation and tilled the ground. Apparently, the ground cursed in Gen 3:17 was not cursed for him. He was able to bring an offering (*minhah*) from the fruit of the ground (not thorns and thistles as the ground was doomed to produce). The word *minhah* derives from the language of gift-giving. In a political setting, it is a gift by which one seeks the goodwill of an overlord, or tribute that pledges one's loyalty to him. In the religious setting, it is an offering, grain or animals, made to God, though in later texts it refers mostly to the grain offering. Both brothers experienced life-supporting produce in their occupations and spontaneously brought gifts of gratitude for the past and prayers for even better results in the future. They were obeying no explicit law; the narrator considers it natural that human beings recognize the creator and his gifts. The same word, *minhah*, is used for both offerings, but the LXX rendered Cain's offering as *thusia*, sacrifice. Jewish and Christian interpreters reading in Greek seize upon this to dwell upon the due qualities of sacrifice and to fault Cain for lacking in them; they note that his sacrifice was not described as of firstlings. The LXX faults Cain for sinning by not rightly dividing his sacrifice. The narrator is, however, silent on this. Abel offered the fatty portions of the firstlings of his flock. The LORD looked with favor on Abel and his offering, but not on Cain and his offering. Theodotion (ca. 150 CE) signifies that fire came from heaven and devoured Abel's offering, but not Cain's, Cassuto that the LORD bestowed fertility upon Abel's flock but not upon Cain's field.[5] Or was Abel's offering accepted because he gave the firstlings and the fattest parts? The

---

5. Cassuto, *Commentary on the Book of Genesis*, 1:207. Westermann, *Genesis 1–11*, 297, concurs: Cain knew it because the blessing was absent.

narrator, however, is silent as to why Abel and his offering found favor, also how they knew God's response. We meet here for the first time in the Bible the mystery of God's election or free choice of the younger over the elder, a theme that drives the plot of many of the Genesis stories.[6] The chosen person is not always more righteous. Does God love all equally? Kaminsky prods reflection when he says that some receive greater gifts than others (see Matt 25:14–30) and asserts that "if God's love is like human love in any way whatsoever, then it is unlikely that God has an identical love for all nations and all individuals."[7] The fact is, some are more favored than others. Many of the factors that matter most in life are unequally distributed.[8] These include internal endowments of mind and body, and external possessions and entitlements. Rather than envy and jealousy, it is best to forge a path to success with what one has at hand.

For Cain, "angry frustration turns into homicidal frustration."[9] He was hot with anger, his countenance fell. He no longer looked up to God nor looked his brother in the eye. This signals a cutting off of normal relationships. The LORD said to Cain, "Why are you angry, and why has your countenance fallen?" (NRSV). The LORD is giving him a chance to take stock of what is happening within him, to reconsider. The next verse runs literally as follows: if you do well, "a lifting up" (see above). The LXX rendered, "Hast thou not sinned if thou hast brought it rightly, but not rightly divided it?" The LXX faults the way Cain made his offering. All the Targums fault Cain and take the obscure śĕʾēt in the sense of 'to forgive.'"[10] For example, Onqelos: "if you do your work well, it will be forgiven you . . . if you do not do your work well, your sin is reserved for the day of judgment, when it will be exacted of you, if you do not convert." The LORD invites him to repentance. However, "lifting up" may refer to Cain's fallen countenance. It may also be the idiom, "to lift up one's face," that is, to accept and honor one. In either case, Cain is being given a path forward, past his resentment to good relations with the LORD and his brother. But if he persists, sin, like a demon or ferocious beast, crouches at the door, ready to pounce. The

---

6. Westermann, *Genesis 1–11*, 297, insists that there is no question here of election or rejection, as these refer to salvation and judgment. According to his view, only *blessing* functions in the secular realm.

7. Kaminsky, "Reclaiming a Theology of Election," 143.

8. Moberly, *Theology of Genesis*, 99.

9. Gunn and Fewell, "Varieties of Interpretation," 28.

10. Vermes, "Targumic Versions of Genesis 4:3–16," 113.

word for sin, *ḥaṭṭaᵭt*, enters the narrative explicitly for the first time, so also the concept of guilt. Resentment, envy, and passion, if given sway, can eat up and destroy a person. The woman's desire shall be for her husband, and he will rule over her (Gen 3:17). Here sin's desire is for you, yet you can rule over it. "At first it [sin] is like a [passing] visitor, then like a guest [who stays longer], and finally like the master of the house."[11] The Lord intones one of the fundamental moral principles: persons have freedom of choice, even in face of compulsions. They need to make sure that an unwelcome visitor does not become master of the house. Moral rectitude entails ongoing struggle against one's inner drives. Cain paid no attention. He lured his brother out to the field to be by themselves and where no one might see, and he killed him there. But the LORD said to him, *where is your brother, Abel?* This is another attempt to awaken Cain's conscience and move him to repentance; it is also a reminder that there is nowhere to hide from the Lord. It is similar to the question "where are you?" said to Adam trying to hide after his transgression. Cain lied: *I do not know; am I my brother's keeper?* "Yes, you are your brother's keeper," the LORD could have retorted. But the LORD patiently laid out the case. *What have you done? The blood of your brother is crying to me from the ground.* The verb *ṣaᵭaq* is usual for the cry of the oppressed, a cry God hears and acts upon. Punishment follows. *Cursed are you from (min) the ground that has drunk your brother's blood.* The same may be rendered, "you are banned from the ground . . ." (NABRE). But it is more likely that the ground is agent of the curse, it will refuse to yield its fruit and so Cain will ever be wandering upon the earth. Traditional societies believe that the ground so reacts against certain heinous crimes, usually through the vengeance of an earth-goddess. Cain is the first person cursed. The snake was cursed from/of (*min*) all animals (Gen 3:14) and so lacks what characterizes other animals.[12] The ground was cursed because of the man (Gen 3:17), so yields for him only thorns and thistles. The curse is a word of power that follows the accursed: "the dissolution which takes place in the soul of the sinner . . . as a poisonous, consuming substance that destroys and undermines, so that the soul falls to pieces and its strength is exhausted."[13] In short, the curse dries up the springs of life generated by blessing. In more traditional societies, fear of

11. *GenR* 22.6: Rabbi Isaac, ca. 150 CE.

12. Cf. Goldingay, *Israel's Gospel*, 140.

13. Pedersen, *Israel: Its Life and Culture*, 2:437.

the power of the curse, especially by an acknowledged righteous person or respected elder, is a potent moral deterrent.

PSALM 133

How good and how pleasant it is. When brothers dwell together as one! Like fine oil on the head, running down upon the beard, upon the beard of Aaron, upon the collar of his robe. Like dew of Hermon coming down upon the mountains of Zion.

There the LORD has decreed a blessing, life for evermore.

Cain said to the LORD, greater is my *'awōn mi-neśō*⊠. The phrase to bear one's *'awōn* can mean to bear one's sin, guilt, or punishment. The LXX rendered, "my guilt is too great for me to be forgiven." The *Fragmentary Targum* has, "my sins are greater than can be borne. Nevertheless there is power before thee to absolve and forgive me." Put so, it is an expression of repentance and plea for pardon. Modern versions tend to read here a plea for the mitigation of the judgment: "my punishment is too great to bear." It is at worship that one sees the face of the LORD, so Blenkinsopp reads Cain's being driven from the face of the Lord as expulsion from the cult community, something that carries with it also loss of civic status.[14] For Cassuto, Cain thought that driven from the ground he would be hidden[15] from the LORD's face, that is, divine protection. A restless vagrant will be liable to death at the hands of anyone who encounters him. The man who has just murdered his brother fears what would happen to him outside the protection of the LORD! But the LORD gives up no one, not even Cain the murderer. Speaking not to Cain but for all to hear, the LORD makes a proclamation: *if anyone kills Cain, Cain shall be avenged seven times.* Sevenfold is not meant literally, rather betokens severity. The LORD put on Cain a sign of protection lest anyone kills him at sight. Cain left the LORD's presence (implies they were face to face) and settled in the land of Nod (Land of Wandering), east of Eden (like Adam banished from the garden).

---

14. Blenkinsopp, *Creation, Un-Creation, Re-Creation*, 96.

15. Cassuto, *Commentary on the Book of Genesis*, 1:223, translates 4:14 as, "and from thy face I shall seek to hide." It is not as if the Lord was God only of the land of Israel. Rather, Cain shall constantly flee from the Lord's presence, only to find him wherever he happens, then fleeing from there also. In other words, he will be haunted by the presence of the Lord. The translation of NABRE, "I must avoid you," presents another face of guilt—avoidance of God and the things of the Holy, in the effort to avoid reckoning.

The Cainites and the Arts and Crafts, Gen 4:17–24

Genesis 4:17–24 traces the line of Cain, while Gen 5:1–32 traces the line of Seth. When the two are compared, it turns out there is a Cainite Enoch and a Sethite Enoch, a Cainite Lamech and a Sethite Lamech, but the profile differs in each case (see the table below). Besides, some of the names sound alike: Irad/Jared; Muthusael/Methuselah.[16] The Cainite genealogy attributes the origins of the arts and crafts to this line, ending with Lamech, the seventh in the line and his three sons (and a daughter); there is narrative focus on Lamech. The Sethite line traces ten generations from Adam to Noah, ending with Noah's three sons; it gives narrative focus to Enoch, the seventh in the line. Some scholars speak of the wicked Cainites and the righteous Sethites; however, all humankind, except the family of Noah (a Sethite) will be characterized as full of violence. Is there hint of something wrong with the Cainite line in the overweening violence of Lamech and the explicit mention of his taking two wives before whom he preens?

Cainite Line, 4:17–22	4:25–26	Sethite Line, 5:1–32	Died at
Adam		Adam	930
Cain	[Abel]/ Seth	Seth	912
Enoch	Enosh	Enosh	905
Irad		Kenan	910
Mehujael		Mahalalel	895
Methusael		Jared	962
		Enoch	365
		Methuselah	969
Lamech		Lamech	777
Jabal Jubal Tubal-Cain Naamah		Noah	950
		Shem Ham Japheth	

CAINITE AND SETHITE GENEALOGIES

By means of a linear genealogy of Cain that becomes segmented with Lamech, the seventh generation, the narrator tells of how people increased

---

16. Scholars debate the prehistory of these genealogies. Most assign Gen 4:17–24 to J and Gen 5:1–32 to P. The majority presume knowledge and editing of Mesopotamian traditions of eight or ten antediluvian kings (on this see the next chapter).

on earth and how various aspects of human culture arose. The culture he-roes are all descended from Lamech. We glean something of the man as he addresses his two wives.[17]

Cain knew his wife and she bore Enoch. Whence Cain's wife, unless an already developed population is presumed?[18] We learn in Gen 5:4 that Adam had other sons and daughters, but this is the Sethite genealogy where Cain does not at all feature. Cain became the founder of a city and named it after his son Enoch. Some scholars emend the text to have Enoch as founder of the city, naming it after himself,[19] but there is no textual support in the ancient versions for this. It arose to close the "gap" caused by the curse of Cain that requires that he be a perpetual wanderer on earth.

A series of names follows—Irad, Mehujael, Methusael, Lamech—that have parallels in the genealogy of Seth in the next chapter (see there). La-mech took two wives, Adah and Zillah. Is this a moral evaluation? Does Lamech's preening before his wives suggest this also? Israel's patriarchs had multiple wives and concubines, so hardly is polygamy being condemned at this stage. Adah gave birth to Jabal, ancestor of those who dwell in tents and keep livestock. Another son, Jubal, was father of those who play the lyre and reed pipe. Zillah birthed Tubal Cain (LXX: Thobel), ancestor of those who forge instruments of bronze and iron. In all this, Israel presents human culture as originating from human inventions and efforts. In the myths of Israel's neighbors, civilization and culture were gifts of the gods. No specific negative note seems to attach to these cultural developments. The city is not evil in itself, nor are implements of bronze and iron necessarily evil in themselves; however, Lamech's violent song raises questions about cultural and technological advances when divorced from morality.[20] One is also given pause by the fact that the entire generation of this Lamech perished in the flood. The other Lamech, father of Noah, the sole survivor with his family, is of the line of Seth. The line of Cain is passed over in favor of that of Seth, another example of the pattern of the elder son being passed over in the line of promise. 1 Enoch (see below) evaluates the cultural developments

17. Some scholars align Cain with the Kenites, an Arabian nomadic tribe who were smiths. This theory is sometimes linked with the Kenite hypothesis in which the Kenites (around Sinai) were YHWH worshipers, a faith they transmitted to Israel. Rowley, *From Joseph to Joshua*, 19–34; Blenkinsopp, "Midianite-Kenite Hypothesis Revisited," 131–53.

18. Unless, of course, Cain were to marry his own sister, which is what we find al-ready in *Jubilees* (second century BCE).

19. Cf. Westermann, *Genesis 1–11*, 319.

20. Blenkinsopp, *Creation, Un-Creation, Re-Creation*, 90.

negatively as part of the efforts of fallen angel Watchers to corrupt humans. Lamech's Song of the Sword is a vignette of primeval wrongdoing. The ancient law of talio is "an eye for an eye, a tooth for a tooth." But Lamech boasts that he killed a youth (synonymous parallelism) for just bruising him. The LORD himself will avenge Cain, but Lamech will himself wreak vengeance, and seventy times that stipulated for Cain. This is violence run riot, with no regard for the fear of God or any constraining power. It depicts what the powerful become when they are a law unto themselves. "Lamech was the first proponent of massive retaliation,"[21] a strategy of war today.

Sethites and YHWH Worship, Gen 4:25–26

Genesis 4:25–26 is a truncated Sethite genealogy, created as suture between the Cainite genealogy in Gen 4:17–24 and the Sethite one in Gen 5:1–32. A give-away sign of the editor's work are the words, "again" (referring back to Gen 4:1–2) and "another" which make room for Seth after Abel: Adam (now a proper name with no definite article) *again* knew his wife who gave birth to Seth, *another* son in place of Abel. Seth begot Enosh, then this genealogy stops dead. Enosh is poetic equivalent of *adam* (humankind) frequent for mortal man over against the immortal divine Being. *Then people began to invoke the LORD by name.* But hasn't the name YHWH been known since Genesis 2 and did not Cain and Abel make offerings to YHWH? Or is it that the worship of YHWH was at first confined to a small group, only later to become the national religion?[22] Cassuto (who rejects the documentary hypothesis) rendered, "then men began once more to call upon the name of the Lord." There is no basis in the text for "once more." The LXX reads a hope for the future: he hoped to invoke the name of the Lord God. Actually the revelation of the name YHWH is given to Moses in Exod 3:13–15 (the Burning Bush, Elohist) and Exod 6:2–3 (Priestly Writer). The Yahwist, however, has YHWH worshiped right from the beginnings of humankind. In his view, religion has always been part of human culture and the God worshiped is in the final analysis YHWH. "The LORD is near to all who call upon him . . . in truth," Ps 145:18. The Bible assumes a natural knowledge of God available to all humanity. This knowledge is couched in the "fear of God" or "fear of YHWH" and associated with moral rectitude.[23]

---

21. Goldingay, *Israel's Gospel*, 155.

22. Speiser, *Genesis*, 37.

23. Levenson, "Universal Horizon of Biblical Particularism," 149.

Theologians distinguish *general revelation* from *special revelation*. That all worship has been of YHWH contains possibilities for interreligious understanding and dialogue. But, why only in the time of Enosh, and not Adam? Or, is Enosh a replica of Adam in the original account?

Tradition

The tradition of Cain as evil and Abel as righteous was fixed before Christianity. The LXX already distinguished evil Cain from righteous Abel; Cain did not rightly divide the sacrifice. For Philo (at the turn of the era) Cain was self-loving and made the offering "after some days," not right away, also "of the fruit," not of the first fruits.[24] He brought inferior crops, like a bad tenant who eats the first ripe figs but honors the king with the late figs.[25] Josephus (ca. 100 CE) relates that Abel was concerned with justice and virtue, while Cain was altogether wicked and on the lookout only for his own profit.[26] Wisd 10:3–4 (ca. 50 BCE) even attributed the flood to him and his line of Cainites: "When an unrighteous man [Cain] withdrew from her [wisdom] in his anger, he perished through his fratricidal wrath. When on his account the earth was flooded, wisdom again saved it, piloting the righteous man on frailest wood." The New Testament picked up the tradition of Cain as evil. 1 John 3:12 says that Cain belonged to the evil one and slaughtered his brother because his own works were evil, and those of his brother righteous.

Levenson suggests that "what Cain cannot bear is a world in which distributive justice is not the highest principle and not every inequity is an iniquity."[27] The Palestinian Targums (*Ps-Jon, Neof, Fragmentary Targums*) on Gen 4:8 record a dispute between Cain and Abel about divine justice in the governance of the world. Cain: the world was not created with divine love and is not arranged in keeping with people's good deeds, for why else would your sacrifice be accepted with favor and mine not? Abel countered: it was because my deeds have been better than yours that my sacrifice was accepted with favor and your sacrifice was not. In the heat of the argu-

---

24. Philo Judaeus, *Sacrifices of Cain and Abel*, 52, cited by Kugel, *Bible as It Was*, 89. In line with this is, Cassuto, *From Adam to Noah*, 205: Cain was indifferent, content merely to discharge the duty; "sacrifices are acceptable only if an acceptable spirit inspires them."

25. *GenR* 22.5.

26. *Ant* 1:53–54.

27. Levenson, *Death and Resurrection of the Beloved Son*, 100n16.

ment, Cain killed his brother Abel. The issues the brothers discussed were possibly current in the targumist's community. The murder is, however, presented as not premeditated. Simeon ben Yohai (ca. 140 CE) even had the LORD say to Cain, "The voice of thy brother's blood cries out against me" (cf. 4:10),[28] that is, for provoking the conflict in the first place! R. Hanin read Cain's words as words of repentance and interpreted the sign to him as making him an example to penitents; the LORD did not put him to death immediately to show the saving power of repentance.[29]

Abel became prototype of martyrs. Jesus warned the scribes and Pharisees to beware lest "there may come upon you all the righteous blood shed upon earth, from the righteous blood of Abel to the blood of Zechariah, son of Berechiah" (Matt 23:35). What distinguished his offering was faith: "by faith Abel offered to God a sacrifice greater than Cain's. Through this he was attested to be righteous, God bearing witness to his gifts" (Heb 11:4). For Augustine, Cain's city symbolizes the earthly city of the joys of the earth, as against Abel who symbolizes the heavenly city in exile on earth.[30] Some Fathers interpret the sign of Cain as bodily tremor and palsied limbs as a lesson for all.[31] The story of Cain and Abel served Martin Luther to illustrate his doctrine of salvation by faith alone. Not the quantity of the work or its quality, but only one's faith draws God's regard. Abel, whose name implies nothingness, makes his offering in the faith of the promise.[32]

In *Jubilees* (second century BCE), Adam and Eve also had two daughters, Awan and Azura: "Cain took Awan his sister to be his wife and she bare him Enoch at the close of the fourth jubilee" (*Jub* 4:9). In other traditions, Cain had a twin sister and Abel two twin sisters;[33] or, one twin sister was born with Abel and they quarreled about who to marry her.[34]

Theodoret of Cyr (393–466) tried to answer those who wondered why God did not seem to punish Lamech. Lamech escaped divine judgment through confession of sin, and pronouncing judgment on himself.

---

28. Reading *'alay* for *'elay* (to me), *GenR* 22.9. God accepts responsibility and regret somewhat?

29. *GenR* 22.12.

30. ACCS, 115, citing *City of God* 15.15.

31. Chrysostom, *Catechetical Lectures*, in ACCS, 108. The LXX had, "Groaning and trembling shall you be upon the earth."

32. Lewis, "Offering of Abel (Gen 4:4)," 493.

33. *GenR* 22.2.

34. *GenR* 22.7.

The tradition of fallen angel Watchers who taught the arts and crafts and corrupted humankind thereby is found in *1 Enoch* 8:1–4.[35]

> Asael taught men to make swords of iron and weapons and shields and breastplates and every instrument of war. He showed them metals of the earth and how they should work gold to fashion it suitably, and concerning silver . . . And there was much godlessness on the earth, and they made their ways desolate. Shemihazah taught spells and the cutting of roots . . . And as men were perishing, the cry went up to heaven.

Onq and *Ps-Jon* both reckon with the fact that YHWH has been acting since Genesis 2 and thus say that in the days of Enosh people ceased praying in the name of the LORD. Rabbi Isaac[36] (150 CE) found here the beginnings of idolatry. People argued, what is the difference whether one worships an image or worships man? Hence, humankind became degraded to worship idols instead of the LORD.

---

35. Text of Nickelsburg and VanderKam, *1 Enoch*, 25–26.

36. The root, *ḥalal*, used here, can in one of its inflections mean "to begin," as if from *yaḥel*, but it has the basic sense of "to profane/pollute." *GenR* 24.6; see also 23.6. *Targum Neofiti* said simply, "then the sons of man began to make idols for themselves and to surname them by the name of the Memra of the Lord." Text from McNamara, *Targum Neofiti 1: Genesis*, 65.

CHAPTER 5

Genesis 5:1—6:4

From Adam to Noah

Introduction

Genesis 6:1–4 is an independent unit that has no grammatical links with the story of the flood. Rather than being the immediate cause of the flood, it is another example in a pattern of transgressions in Genesis 1–11, each calling forth the divine response. The hundred and twenty years are not a respite period before the flood, but a limitation to the span of human life.

The Sethite Genealogy

The Sethite genealogy in Genesis 5 covers ten generations, from creation to the flood: from Adam, through Seth, to Noah and his three sons. The Sumerian King List which begins with, "when kingship was lowered from heaven,"[1] counted eight antediluvian kings, demi-gods. The Babylonian King List, as in the late third century BCE Greek work of the Babylonian priest Berossus, had ten antediluvian kings who were also sages. The kings in question lived very long lives, totaling 432,000; one king, EnmenluAnna, ruled for 43,200 years. The years of rule decrease drastically after the deluge. The antediluvians in the biblical text also have long life spans (though none reached a thousand years) which generally decrease after the flood. Enmeduranki is seventh in line in the King Lists. He was loved by the gods who made him an associate, seating him on the left of the throne, revealing

1. *ANET*, 265.

to him all secrets, and consigning to him the tablets of the gods.[2] The profile of Enoch, the seventh generation after Adam, is similar. Enmeduranki is associated with Sippar, city of the sun-god; Enoch lived three hundred and sixty-five years, parallel to the number of days in a solar year. The parallels between Enmeduranki and Enoch increase in the Pseudepigrapha, for example, *1 Enoch*. The biblical author may have redirected[3] an old myth to a new purpose, the transmission of the image and likeness of God, without at the same time confusing the boundary between the human and the divine.

Scholars grapple with how to harmonize the life spans of the antediluvians with the date of the flood. The LXX (2,244 years) and the Samaritan Pentateuch (1,307 years) differ from the Hebrew Text (1,656 years) both in the life spans and the total number of years before the flood. However, Noah is the goal in the three accounts, which all seem to count backwards from him. Augustine noted that no one has ventured to correct the LXX from the Hebrew text, for the numbers were not considered falsification, rather "we should believe that they were moved by the Holy Spirit to say something differently."[4] Jerome had to answer those who calculated that Methuselah must have lived fourteen years after the flood. After a wearisome computation, he concluded that he must have died in the very year the flood began.[5]

Genesis 5 begins with a recapitulation of Genesis 1, recalling that Elohim created humankind, male and female, in God's likeness, and called them *adam*/humankind. That God called them *adam*/humankind is new information; it may stress that they remain human despite the likeness to God. At a hundred and thirty years, Adam (now a proper name) *begot a son in his likeness, after his image, and called him Seth*. Goldingay takes this to mean that the offspring resemble their parents, not the creator.[6] The inverse seems to be the case: they are like Adam who is like God. Seth is the direct line from Adam in this genealogy; there is no mention of Cain. The author may have wanted to reestablish humankind on less ambiguous basis than that of a murderer. The genealogy manifests the fruit of the blessing of God: human beings increase on the earth, they beget sons and daughters. The pattern of narration is as follows: years till the first son, years after, then

2. Cf. Cassuto, *From Adam to Noah*, 282.

3. Ibid., 262.

4. *City of God* 15.14, in ACCS, 122.

5. *Hebrew Questions on Genesis*, in ACCS, 121.

6. Goldingay, *Israel's Gospel*, 159.

the total number of years at death. Each line ends with "*then he died*," making the account of Enoch that lacks this phrase stand out. Adam had other sons and daughters; does this explain Cain's wife? There is here no narrative focus on Enosh as in Gen 4:25–26.

Enoch walked with God after he begot Methuselah. The name Enoch derives from the root, *ḥanak*, which means "to dedicate." To "walk with God" is idiom for righteous and holy living. The same phrase will be used of Noah in Gen 6:9, and a similar phrase used of Levi in Mal 2:6. LXX said simply that Enoch was pleasing to God. Interpretive traditions will query whether he always walked with God or did so only *after* he begot Methuselah. His life span of three hundred and sixty-five years (the number of days in the solar calendar) was the shortest. Again interpreters will wonder why. Of Enoch alone is the formula, "*and he died*," not repeated, rather *he was no longer here for God took him*. The same verb, *laqaḥ*, is used of the translation of Elijah in 2 Kgs 2:11–12. Our text seems to explain the absence of Enoch in terms of his being translated by God. LXX has, "and he was not found, because God transferred him." Like Enoch, righteous and holy persons belong to God so completely that God enfolds them and draws them to himself.

Lamech *begot a son and named him Noah*. But he interpreted the name as if it were Menahem, with the root, *niḥam*, to comfort, not *nuaḥ*, to rest. Lamech's prophecy looks forward to Gen 8:21 (withdrawal of the curse on the ground) and Noah's planting of a vineyard (Gen 9:20). The Sethite genealogy ends with the birth of Shem, Ham, and Japheth; this will be picked up at 6:9 at the beginning of the account of the flood.

The Sons of God and the Daughters of Humankind

The short unit of Gen 6:1–4 bristles with difficulties. This is partly because aspects of a mythic background seem to have been repurposed and given new ethical functions. Ben Sira 16:7, "he did not forgive the princes of old who rebelled long ago in their might," interprets this text in terms of a rebellion against God with the flood as due punishment, an interpretation that links Gen 6:1–4 with what follows.

There are three chief interpretative paths for the phrase "sons of God."[7] First, they are Sethites, while the daughters of humankind are Cainites.

---

7. For this summary, I am indebted to Clines, "Significance of the 'Sons of God' Episode," 33–46.

However, this would mean that *ha-adam* (humankind) would have two different senses in 6:1 and 6:2. Second, the sons of God are heavenly beings who mated with earthly women. A problem would be that humankind is punished while the culprits escape punishment; another would be the saying in Matt 22:30 that the risen neither marry nor are given in marriage but are like the angels in heaven. Lastly, the sons of God are dynastic rulers, oriental despots who establish royal harems by force or practice indiscriminate rape. In this scenario, the punishment of humankind is more intelligible since peoples were often punished for the crimes of their rulers, however, rulers are not called "sons of God" in narrative, only rarely so in court language and poetry. I interpret "sons of God" as heavenly beings. In the Canaanite context, "sons of God" always referred to the lesser gods of the pantheon, members of the divine council. This meaning occurs in several places in the Hebrew Bible, for example, Deut 32:8, "when the Most High allotted each nation its heritage . . . he set up the boundaries of peoples after the number of the divine beings" (literally, "sons of God"). On the function of the unit, I agree with Petersen[8] that along with Gen 3:22 it explains why people do not, regularly, live more than a hundred and twenty years, and what the origin of the men of renown was. YHWH's action in Gen 3:22 is threatened by the intervention of the sons of the gods! He must again act to prevent humanity from gaining immortality, thereby preserving the boundary between human and divine.

When human beings began to grow on the earth and daughters were born to them. The narrator focuses on the women as having an important role in the drama to unfold. The bipolar contrast of sons/daughters, of God/ of humankind suggests that the sons of God belong outside the sphere of humankind. But how can spiritual beings mate with women? Westermann interprets sons of God as superior and powerful persons restrained by no limits.[9] For him the story is about the human phenomenon of "what happens when an encounter with beauty goes beyond the bounds which ought not be overstepped."[10] Against this can be said that the context knew divine-human unions and persons who are both human and divine. Gilgamesh was two-thirds divine and one-third human.

---

8. Petersen, "Genesis 6:1–4," 54, 57.

9. Westermann, *Genesis 1–11*, 367.

10. Ibid., 371. Because the story is told in primeval time, when there were yet no social and political classes, these persons are referred to as divine beings, the only beings then superior to humans. Like eating your cake and having it?

The sons of God *saw the daughters of humans that they were good/ ṭōbōt*. In Genesis 1, after endowing each creation with attributes for its well-being and the well-being of others, "God saw that it was good." In the text before us, otherworldly beings saw the women that they were good (desirable for their own purposes) and *they took for their wives whomever they pleased* (NABRE); this translation may suggest force. The verb *laqaḥ* is normal for the legal process of taking a woman to wife, though the juxtaposition of "saw . . . took" may suggest unrestrained use of power without any reckoning. The NJB suggests promiscuity: they married *as many of them as they chose*. The children of the angel-human unions could be expected to live forever or/and be superhuman in some form. The LORD intervenes to prevent such happening: *my spirit shall not remain in human beings forever, because they are only flesh.*[11] The breath (*neshamah*, Gen 2:7) of the LORD made humankind a living being. As long as humans have in them this breath (here called *ruaḥ*), they live. The LORD decides to limit the life span to a hundred and twenty years.[12] The attempt to cross the boundary between human and divine is frustrated, so these offspring remain flesh, that is, human and not divine. The situation thus resembles God's action in Gen 3:22 that shut off the tree of life lest the man eat of it and live forever.

The author then makes a conscious effort to dissociate himself from aspects of the myth. Rather than say that the offspring of the unions were the Nephilim and the *gibborim* (heroes/giants), he dissimulated and said that *the Nephilim appeared on the earth in those days* when the sons of God went in to the daughters of humankind and had offspring by them. A correction, "*as well as later*," takes account of the report of the twelve scouts in Num 13:33, that in Canaan they saw the Nephilim before whom they seemed like mere grasshoppers. How did they survive the flood? The word Nephilim derives from the verb *naphal*, to fall. It is the *qatil* form that means "those who were made to fall, those who were cast down."[13] Does this retain some memory of fallen heavenly beings causing havoc on earth?

---

11. This translation follows the LXX in reading *yādūr* (dwell, abide) instead of *yādōn* (contend). NJB: My spirit cannot indefinitely be responsible for human beings, who are only flesh.

12. A problem is that people continued to live much longer than this stipulation. Accordingly, many scholars interpret 120 years as period of respite before the flood, just as in the Atrahasis Epic 1200 years intervened between catastrophes that climaxed in the flood. See Clines, "Significance of the 'Sons of God' Episode," 42.

13. Hamilton, *Genesis, Chapters 1–17*, 269.

As the text is, only the heroes/giants are identified as men of renown, but neither is explicitly identified with the Nephilim.

Tradition

That Enoch walked with God *after* begetting Methuselah seemed to suggest that he was not pious before that. Ben Sira 44:16 (LXX) had him repent: "and he was changed, an example of repentance for generations." Philo says that not very long after the forgiving of Cain, Scripture introduces the fact that Enoch repented, informing us that forgiveness produces repentance.[14] And why was his life span so short? "He pleased God and was loved by him, but lived among sinners. Perfected in a short time, he was transported by the Lord, snatched away lest wickedness pervert his mind or deceit beguile his soul" (Wisdom 4:10–11).

The most common tradition interprets *and he was not, for God took him* to mean that Enoch never saw death, and that already in LXX. This tradition appears in Heb 11:5, "by faith Enoch was taken up so that he should not see death." However, had God not decreed death for all humankind? So, some traditions leave the matter ambiguous. *Targum Neofiti* says, "and it is not known where he was withdrawn by a command from before the Lord." *Onqelos* says bluntly: "then he was no more for the Lord had caused him to die." Tertullian records a tradition that has the transported Elijah and Enoch come back to die one day that they may extinguish Antichrist with their blood.[15] In this, Tertullian takes Elijah and Enoch to be the two witnesses martyred in Revelation 11.

Jewish and Christian traditions generally interpreted the sons of God as angels of God (LXX, Philo, *Questions and Answers in Genesis*, *1 Enoch*). Josephus relates that many angels of God consorted with women and brought forth wanton children, children who were disdainful of all good because of their overweening trust in brute strength.[16] 2 Peter 2:4 speaks of angels who sinned and were condemned to the chains of Tartarus, though the nature of the sin is not identified. This is what Jude 6–7 does:

> The angels too, who did not keep to their own domain but deserted their proper dwelling, he has kept in eternal chains, in gloom, for

---

14. *Questions and Answers in Genesis*, 1.82.

15. *On the Soul*, 50.5, in ACCS, 121.

16. *Ant* 1.73. See Kugel, *Bible as It Was*, 112.

the judgment of the great day. Likewise, Sodom, Gomorrah . . . which in the same manner as they, indulged in sexual promiscuity and practiced unnatural vice . . .

What Jude mentions here is detailed in *1 Enoch* 6–11 (see citation at the end of the last chapter) and *Jubilees* 4–5. The Fathers of the church followed this interpretation. Clement of Alexandria (second century CE) speaks of the angels who forsook the beauty of God for perishable beauty and fell as far as heaven is from the earth.[17] Ambrose says that the giants (Nephilim) were generated by angels and women. However, from the second century CE, a reaction set in among Jewish and Christian interpreters.[18] Simeon ben Yohai (ca. 140 CE) insisted that the sons of God were sons of nobles and cursed all who called them sons of God.[19] In fact, the Targums generally call them "the sons of the mighty" (*Onqelos*), "the sons of the great" (*Ps-Jonathan*), "the sons of the judges"[20] (*Neofiti*). Among Christians, Ephrem the Syrian (fourth century CE), followed by Augustine, interpreted the sons of God as Sethites who abandoned their holiness and sank down into the city of men and begot giants.[21]

Targum Neofiti and *Ps-Jonathan* read Gen 6:3a as "my spirit shall not judge . . . ," reading *yādīn* for *yādōn* (contend). They distinguished the generation of the deluge from other generations: "none of the generations yet to arise will be judged according to the order of the generation of the Flood . . ." (*Neofiti*). The reason is that the generation of the flood perpetrated evil deeds despite receiving the Holy Spirit of God. The Targums all interpret the hundred and twenty years as period of respite for the sake of repentance. For example, *Onqelos*: "I will extend them a hundred and twenty years if they may be converted." Ephrem the Syrian and Jerome are among the Fathers of the church who take the hundred and twenty years as time for people to repent and be saved from the coming wrath.[22]

17. *Christ the Educator*, 3.2.14, in ACCS, 124.

18. Maher, *Targum Pseudo-Jonathan to Genesis*, notes to Gen 6:1, suggests this was perhaps a reaction to esoteric groups that gave excessive importance to angels.

19. *GenR* 24.5.

20. Of the slave who wishes to stay with his master, Exod 21:6 says, "the master shall bring him to God (Elohim)." Some scholars argue that Elohim here means judges. See also at Exod 22:7–8.

21. Augustine, *City of God*, 15.23, in ACCS, 125.

22. See ACCS, 125.

CHAPTER 6

Genesis 6:5—8:22

The Flood

> *Noah, found just and perfect, renewed the race in the time of devastation.*
>
> —BEN SIRA 44:17

Introduction

"The flood is the archetype of human catastrophe."[1] It is God's absolute "no" to a corrupt and violent world. However, its function is not only judgment, rather "the intention of the stories is to overcome the anxiety that there could ever be such a cosmic catastrophe as punishment from the gods or from the creator God."[2] Isaiah 54:9–10 illustrates this point when it invokes the days of Noah to reassure exiled Israel of the divine commitment.

ISAIAH 54:9–10

This is for me like the days of Noah: As I swore then that the waters of Noah should never again flood the earth, so I have sworn now not to be angry with you, or to rebuke you. Though the mountains fall away and the hills be shaken, my love shall never fall away from you nor my covenant of peace be shaken, says the Lord, who has mercy on you.

Narrative criticism sometimes profits from a look at the prehistory of the text, for, as I wrote in chapter 1 under "Narrative Approach," "the text itself has had a history and there may be textual riddles to be

1. Westermann, *Genesis 1–11*, 398.
2. Zenger and Lönig, "World as the House of the Merciful God," 119.

deciphered and apparent contradictions to be resolved. A synchronic reading thus cannot dispense with all historical or source-oriented inquiries." This is definitely the case for the biblical flood story. Scholars usually divide the account into the Yahwist and Priestly sources. Habel[3] speaks rather of the *Adamah* Flood Myth and the *Erets* Flood Myth, the one focusing on animals and birds (reptiles, sea creatures or any types of flora not considered), the other on the earth and all *basar*/flesh. The analysis below shows clearly that two accounts have been dovetailed.

	The *Adamah* Flood Myth	The *Erets* Flood Myth
Rationale for the Flood		
Situation	Great wickedness of *adam*	All *basar* with corrupted ways
Divine Reaction	YHWH sorry	Elohim communicates with Noah
Divine Decision	YHWH to blot out *adam*	Elohim to destroy all *basar/flesh*
Overreaction	To blot out all on *adamah*	Elohim to destroy *erets*/earth
Divine Afterthought	Noah finds grace	Noah found righteous
Decision to Save Species		
Concerning the Ark	Noah to enter ark	Noah to make ark as specified
Species specified	7 clean, 2 unclean	2 of each kind
Reason given	To keep seed alive	Covenant with Noah to keep alive
Extent of the Flood	Blot out life on *adamah*	Destroy all *basar* under the sky
Advent of the Flood		
Boarding of Ark	Noah and animals board	Noah, family, 2 of each kind
Date of the Flood		17.2.600 of Noah's life
Source of the Flood	40 days and nights of rain	Fountains of deep and windows of sky
Extent of the Flood		
Flooding	On earth 40 days	Mighty waters for 150 days
Extent	Lifts ark above earth	Rises 15 cubits above mountains
Species	All life on *adamah* dies	All *basar* on *erets* expires
Termination of the Flood		
Timing	At end of 40 days	At end of 150 days
Cause	Rains cease from sky closed	Wind blows on *erets*, fountains and windows
Evidence of end	Noah sends dove and raven	Ark rests on mountains of Ararat
Closing scenario	Dove does not return	Animals depart to multiply
After the Flood	Noah sees *adamah* is dry	Noah and family leave ark 27.2.601 of Noah's life

3. Habel, *The Birth, the Curse and the Greening of Earth*, 93.

ADAMAH AND *ERETS* MYTHS

Parallels with and differences from flood stories in the Mesopotamian context throw light on the function of the biblical story and its parts. Mesopotamian stories of the flood are extant in the Gilgamesh Epic discovered in the 1849–1854 excavation of the library of Asshurbanipal in Nineveh. Concerned with the inevitability of death, these poems go back to a third millennium Sumerian model; Tablet XI deals with the flood. When his friend Enkidu dies, Gilgamesh set off to the ends of the earth (land of Dilmun) to the ancestor, Utnapishtim, and his wife, who told the story of a flood in which they alone survived and were made immortal. Another flood story is the Atrahasis Epic, an old Babylonian recension copied in 1692 BCE from an earlier text. Atrahasis, meaning "most wise," is an epithet of Utnapishtim. The flood is one of many disasters visited upon humankind with the goal of reducing the human population and so decreasing the uproar and clamor that were disturbing the sleep of the gods. It is not clear whether uproar and clamor signify some type of rebellion. There is finally the account of Berossus, a priest of Marduk in Babylon around 275 BCE, from a three-volume history of Babylon, from creation to Alexander the Great, that survives only in quotations in other works. The hero of this account is Xisuthros, the tenth in the royal line. Contact with such Mesopotamian models may explain the uncommon number of *hapax legomena* or rare words in the biblical account: *gofer* (rendered gopherwood; translators are not sure what this is), *qinnim* (cells), *kofer* (pitch = Akkadian *kupru*), *ṣohar* (opening for daylight), *taraph* (fresh-plucked), *mabbul* (upper waters; elsewhere only Ps 29:10), *yeqūm* (existence).

Here are some striking parallels.[4]

---

4. For the parallels and differences, see Heidel, *Gilgamesh Epic*, 225–69.

Table 5: Parallels

Xisuthros is tenth in (royal) line (Berossus account)	Noah is tenth generation from Adam
A god drew the plan of the ship	Detailed divine specifications of the ark
The flood is universal and exterminated humans and other living things	The flood is universal and exterminated humans and other living things
Utnapishtim completed the building of the ship in seven days	Seven days from now I will bring rain down on the earth, Gen 7:4
Utnapishtim sent dove—swallow—raven	Noah sent raven—dove—dove—dove, 8:6–12
Utnapishtim built an altar and offered sacrifices and libation	Noah built an altar and offered burnt offerings
the gods smelled the savor . . . the gods crowded like flies about the sacrifice	the Lord smelled the pleasing odor, 8:20, 21
Enlil blessed Utnapishtim	Elohim/God blessed Noah and his sons
Marduk suspended his bow in the sky (Enuma Elish)—not part of a flood story	(rain)bow in sky is sign of eternal covenant, Gen 9:16

Here are some differences.[5]

---

5. These point to a resignification of the function of the biblical narrative. The flood acquires an explicitly moral motivation. The punishment fits the crime: the whole earth is corrupt, except one man (with his family) and so they merit what they got.

Table 6: Differences: Atrahasis and Bible

Flood is one of many disasters designed to curtail human population	explicit moral motivation for the flood, Gen 6:5–6
destroying gods in conflict with sparing god (Ea/Enki)	the one God is destroyer and sustainer; the conflict is in the heart of God
Ziusudra said to be pious and god-fearing, though not explicit this was why he was saved (only in the Sumerian account)	Noah is saved because righteous; implies the guilt of all the others
Noise and uproar of humans disturbed the sleep of the gods	sin of the flood generation was violence, social injustice
the hero himself shut the door of the ark	The Lord shut Noah in the ark
Utnapishtim built a huge ship and employed a steersman	ark is like a box, has no rudder/sail; deliverance due to God alone
Ship has seven storeys, an exact cube	ark has three storeys, a box
flood waters cease of themselves	flood waters cease when God remembered Noah, 8:1
a great number saved	eight persons saved: Noah, three sons, wives
grounded on Mount Nisir (mount of salvation)	grounded on one of the mountains of Ararat
protest of Ea after the flood: "on the sinner impose his sin, on the transgressor impose his transgression"— flood came on good and evil alike	every desire their heart conceived was always evil, 6:5; all mortals had corrupted their ways on the earth, 6:12—flood was on a deserving world
Utnapishtim granted immortality by the gods and settled in Dilmun	Noah remains mortal, works the earth

Divine Response to Massive Corruption and Violence

The flood is not a capricious act of God, rather a massive divine response to evil gone riot, for *great was the evil of humankind on earth*. Two rationales are given for this. *Every* desire [*yēṣer*] of the heart of humankind was *nothing but evil*—"every" and "nothing but evil" (6:5) highlighting how the whole fabric was eaten up. Second, *the desires of the human heart are evil from youth* (8:21). Hyperbole is sometimes used to underline the greatness or gravity of a situation. When God tells the prophet to roam Jerusalem to find even one who acts justly and God will pardon the city (Jer 5:1), was it that not one just person could be found? Similarly here, were even babies guilty? Or was it that in this period questions were not yet raised about children suffering the fate of their fathers?

The Lord regretted making human beings on the earth and his heart was grieved. The omniscient narrator informs us of how the Lord felt—regret and pain. The divine heartache over creation shows "a God who is so vulnerable to human unrighteousness, who can be hurt by human sin."[6] The same pain (root ☒ṣb) the Lord inflicted on man's labor and woman's childbearing (Gen 3:16, 17) now afflicts God's own heart. Regret is the emotion of one taken by surprise at how things have turned out.[7] This seems to contradict divine immutability in Greek thought in which every change implies imperfection, and God is perfect. So, the LXX avoided the term "repented," to render: "then the Lord considered that he had made humankind on the earth, and he thought over it." But does God change or repent? A sincere relationship is one in which those engaged in it respond to each other: "how people respond to God *matters* to God, and *affects* how God responds to people."[8] Why is the option of forgiveness not open, considering the real pain as that of a father or mother? God addressed only Noah, never the generation of the flood, nor were they warned about what was about to happen or given time to repent. Is it that God respects human choices or that habitual wrongdoing so hardens the soul (the Pharaoh of Exodus is a case in point) as to close the door to the gentle inspirations

---

6. Mann, *Book of the Torah*, 22.

7. Fretheim, "God of the Flood Story," 32, comments that we might suggest that God's regret assumes that God did not know for sure that this would happen (as elsewhere— see Gen 22:12; Deut 8:2). This does not mean that God is not omniscient; God knows all there is to know, including all possibilities, but there is a future that is not yet available for knowing, even for God. For detail, see also Fretheim, *Suffering of God*, 45–59.

8. Moberly, "Does God Change?," in *Old Testament Theology*, 107–43, here 121.

of grace and eventually to repentance? Anyway, there is no indication of repentance by the generation of the flood; besides, in the early period of Israelite religion, even repentance at best mitigates or postpones punishment, it does not obviate it.[9] It will take the drama of the Golden Calf (Exod 32) to raise the question of true forgiveness.

The divine response is to wipe human beings off the *adamah*/ground, and with them the animals, birds, and crawling things. The phrase *"whom I created"* pinpoints the pain of a workman destroying his own work! The verb *mahah* means "to wipe clean": humankind has become a terrible memory the LORD wishes to erase, except for Noah and his family, eight in all. Were they too few to save the rest, seeing that the LORD will be prepared to spare Sodom and Gomorrah were there ten righteous in it (Gen 18:32)?

In a second rationale, Gen 6:11–13, the narrator informs that *the earth was corrupt in the view of God and full of lawlessness* [*hamas*, violence], for *all flesh had corrupted their ways on earth.* "Flesh" includes all living beings, not just humans. One's way (*derek*) is the driving characteristic, one's essential nature. Corrupting their ways means that "humans are not being genuinely human, hawks are not being hawks, and ants are not being true to their nature as ants."[10] Since God says in Gen 9:5 that he will demand an accounting from animals that take life, we are to think of beasts giving up eating vegetables, as prescribed in Gen 1:29, to kill each other and humans. *Hamas* is the violent breach of a just order, "virtually a technical term for the oppression of the weak by the strong."[11] This may hint at traditions, preserved in books like *1 Enoch*, where the offspring of the sons of God began to cause havoc on earth. It is remarkable that the accusation is not idolatry, but socio-moral crimes. That God holds society accountable for the misdeeds of its persons was revolutionary in the ancient world.[12] In the context of evolutionary theory, Spero thinks of the violence of dinosaurs and such beings destroying everything in their path and necessitating "a mid-course correction of the evolutionary process; a divine intervention by means of mass extinctions of unwanted species followed by a selected survival of more benign forms of life."[13] In Gen 1:31, God saw all he had created and behold it was very good; now God saw the earth and behold it was

---

9. Milgrom, "Repentance," 737.

10. Habel, *Ecological Reading of Genesis 1–11*, 86.

11. Goldingay, *Israel's Gospel*, 165.

12. Sarna, *Understanding Genesis*, 51.

13. Spero, "Why Was God Optimistic after the Flood?," 238.

corrupt! God responds measure for measure: they *hishḥitu* (ruin, pervert, corrupt) the earth; behold me *mashhitam* (ruining, corrupting) them along with the earth. In this text, the earth is regarded merely as humankind's environment, so ruined with it; modern sensitivity to the earth as a subject of rights poses questions about such treatment.

The LORD Singles Out Noah

But Noah found favor with the LORD. Did he find favor because he was just? The text hastens to affirm that *Noah was a righteous man and blameless in his generation; Noah walked with God,* just as Gen 5:24 reported of Enoch. He lived his life in conscious obedience to what pleased God. The just person, *ṣaddiq*, fulfills all obligations within a relationship, be it with God, with persons, or the community. But, what if Noah, like Abraham, had argued with God on behalf of the children?"[14] Rather, he simply followed directions and exhibited "no qualms or feelings for his fellow creatures."[15] In fact, all through the drama, Noah never speaks!

God directed Noah to prepare an ark of wood and gave specifications. The word for ark is *tēbah*, which occurs again only for the papyrus basket that saved Moses from the waters (Exod 2:3). It is to have three compartments and be covered inside and outside with pitch. God is about to bring on the *mabbul* (Gen 6:17), that is, the ocean above, to destroy *all flesh in which there is the breath of life.* Humans and all living things survive on the breath of life; all of them will expire. This apparently does not include what lives in the seas or under the earth. While all on the ground expire, *I will establish my covenant with you* and your family, that is, to preserve you from harm and make you the start of a new humankind. Of all living creatures, Noah is to take a male and a female to preserve them. This becomes in Gen 7:2–3 seven pairs of the clean animals, a pair of the unclean, and seven pairs of every bird of the air (for this discrepancy, see above). The greater number of animals provides for the sacrifice Noah will make later. Although the text is anthropocentric, the concern to preserve other living beings than humans accords them value. The text does not raise the question of how representatives of all living beings can be herded into one place or the amount of food they would need. This is primeval history in which images communicate profound truths of existence. *For seven days*

14. Fretheim, "God of the Flood Story," 21.
15. Humphreys, *Character of God in Genesis,* 68.

from now, I will bring rain down on the earth for forty days and forty nights. In the parallel account, *all the fountains of the great abyss burst forth, and the floodgates of the sky were opened* (Gen 7:11). When God created the heavens and the earth, he put in a dome to separate the waters above (the *mabbul*) from the waters below (abyss) to allow the ground to emerge as living space. Now, in an act of uncreation, he reverses the process and returns all to *tohu wa-bohu* (watery wilderness)! *Then the LORD shut him in.* An act of parental loving care. The narrator repeatedly informs us that Noah *did just as God had commanded him.* This underlines the forethought and providence of God, also that righteousness is founded on obedience to the word of God. In one account, the flood lasted forty days (Gen 7:12, 17), in another, a hundred and fifty days (Gen 7:24); for this discrepancy, see above. The Lord achieved his purpose: except for Noah and family and all with him in the ark, *he wiped out every being on earth.*

God Remembered Noah

God remembered Noah and all the animals (Gen 8:1). This is the turning point. As at Jonah 4:11 ("not to mention the animals") the divine memory includes the animals, now accorded value in themselves. When God remembers, he acts, sets things in motion. In the first creation, a wind of God (*ruah Elohim*) was sweeping over the waters (Gen 1:2), now Elohim made a wind (*ruah*) sweep over the earth, and the waters began to subside. The fountains of the abyss (*Tehom* as in Gen 1:2) were stopped, the floodgates of the sky were closed. At the end of a hundred and fifty days, the ark came to rest on the mountains of Ararat (Arartu in North-West Iraq). Noah sent out a couple of birds till the dove came back to him with a plucked-off olive tree, a signal that the waters had abated. He waited seven days and released the dove, but this time it did not return. Then God commanded Noah to leave the ark with his family and the three categories of beasts, birds and creeping things. Then just as in the first creation God blessed Noah and all the animals with him, conferring the power to increase and multiply on the earth. God's blessing reassures the repopulation of the earth.

The first thing Noah did on leaving the ark was to build an altar to the LORD and offer holocausts of every clean animal and clean bird. Scholars debate whether this was a sacrifice of propitiation or one of thanksgiving for safety. I agree with Mann[16] that it was "an act of reverent gratitude,"

---

16. Mann, *Book of the Torah,* 23.

at the same time "the first and only expressed desire within the primeval cycle for reconciliation with God." Was the Mosaic distinction of clean and unclean projected backward? Not necessarily, for most ancient cultures observe a system of clean and unclean animals, taboos of certain species believed to be dangerous to the community because not acceptable to the god?[17] *The LORD smelled the sweet odor.* When the surviving hero of the flood in the Gilgamesh Epic offered sacrifice, "the gods smelled the savor, the gods smelled the sweet savor, the gods crowded like flies about the sacrifice."[18] Those gods were starved; sacrifice in ancient religion was the food of the gods! Biblical religion retains the formula to describe a sacrifice pleasing to God. The Lord's response to the pleasing sacrifice returns to the language of "heart." In Gen 6:6, the narrator told us how the LORD's view of humankind was painful *to his heart*; here the loyal thanksgiving of Noah caused the Lord to assuage his heart (literally: say *to his heart*).[19] The Lord makes a pledge to himself, but the narrator lets the reader in on the secret.

> *Never again will I curse the ground because of human beings, since the desires of the human heart are evil from youth; nor will I ever again strike down every living being, as I have done.* (8:21)

The very reason for the flood (Gen 6:5) is now given for the promise of never again! This implies that "the Great Flood is a demonstration of power and might, but in the end it is a wash."[20] The desires of the human heart remain evil from youth, just as before. So what has changed? "The Flood did not transform the human being, but God."[21]

> Just because the world now stands under the divine mercy, the Flood is unrepeatable. It is not that the reason for the Flood no longer exists, as if the wickedness of the generation of the Flood was greater than that of any subsequent generation. Mankind after the Flood is not different; the Flood has not improved man . . . In spite of the motivation for a flood remaining present, God binds himself to take another course of action.[22]

---

17. Westermann, *Genesis 1–11*, 428.

18. *ANET*, 95.

19. See Alter, *Genesis: Translation and Commentary*, 36.

20. Humphreys, *Character of God in Genesis*, 73.

21. Zenger and Loning, "World as House of the Merciful Father," 124.

22. Clines, "Theology of the Flood Narrative," 139–140.

God decides to go with a wicked world, come what may. In committing to an imperfect world, God determines to take suffering into his own self and bear it for the sake of the future of the world.[23] In Gen 3:17 the Lord said, "Cursed [*arûrah*] is the ground because of you!" Here he lifts that curse (using *qalal*, treat lightly or with disdain) and liberates the ground from sharing in any punishment of humankind—in short, he makes the ground again a subject of rights. There is no longer any divine curse on the ecosystems of climate and of weather.[24]

The LORD then proceeds to formalize this in a covenant with creation: *all the days of the earth, seedtime and harvest, cold and heat, summer and winter, and day and night, shall not cease.* In short, God will allow the appointed order to continue. Does "all the days of the earth" hint at the world coming to an end sometime, or is this a promise that it will never end, the judgment in the flood being the worst destruction the world would ever see?[25]

Tradition

The question "Does God change or repent?" was one that exercised the mind of ancient interpreters, especially in areas of Greek culture. Philo deemed it a great act of wickedness to think that the unchangeable God can be changed.[26] For Rashi, the thoughts of God turned from divine mercy to divine justice. The Targums, however, translated regret literally. Only the grief did they dissimulate: "and he was determined to break their power according to his will" (*Onqelos*); "and he got impatient and was quieted in his heart" (*Neofiti*); "and he debated in his Memra about them" (*Pseudo-Jonathan*). Some rabbis took the regret seriously and had God accept a measure of responsibility. Rabbi Aibu (fourth century): it was a regrettable error on my part to have created an evil urge (*yēṣer ha-ra'*) within him, for had I not created an evil urge within him he would not have rebelled against me.[27] Augustine[28] insists that God's "anger" implies no perturbation of the divine mind. When God "thinks and then has second thoughts" this merely means

23. Fretheim, "God of the Flood Story," 33.
24. Habel, *Ecological Reading of Genesis 1–11*, 196.
25. Kreider, "Flood as Bad as It Gets," 419.
26. *Unchangeableness of God*, 5:22.
27. *GenR* 27.4.
28. *City of God*, 15.22, in ACCS, 128.

that changeable realities come into relation with his immutable reason. For God cannot "repent" as human beings repent, since in regard to everything his judgment is as fixed as his foreknowledge is clear. Here biblical language is in some conflict with dogmatic language; the text does show God as open to change and to do things in new ways in view of new experiences with the world.[29]

What does Noah being righteous *in his generation* mean? The LXX rendered the text: Noah was a righteous man, being perfect in his era. Josephus dramatized his righteousness; he had Noah in vain try to persuade the sons of God and their offspring to change their conduct, and afraid they would kill him and family, he departed from that land.[30] However, disputes with the church about circumcision and justification may have led to a denigration of Noah. *Targum Neofiti* says "because he was not just."[31] *Onqelos* rendered: "but Noah found mercy before the Lord"—spared though unworthy.

BEN SIRA 44:17–18

Noah, found just and perfect, renewed the race in the time of devastation. Because of his worth there were survivors, and with a sign to him the deluge ended. A lasting covenant was made with him that never again would all flesh be destroyed.

Two second-century CE Tannaim differed.[32] For Rabbi Judah, only in his generation was Noah a righteous man; Rabbi Nehemiah: if he was righteous even in his generation, how much more so had he lived in the age of Moses.

What was the sin of the generation of the flood? The targumic tradition is united in defining it as acts of robbery (*Onqelos, Ps-Jonathan*) or that "the earth was filled with violent men and robberies before them" (*Neofiti*).

Why the wait of seven days in Gen 7:4? They were seven days in which the Holy One mourned for his world before bringing the flood. That is, to

---

29. Fretheim, "God of the Flood Story," 28.

30. *Ant* I.74

31. See Okoye, "Genesis 1–11 in the Pseudo-Jonathan Targum," 42. McNamara in *Targum Neofiti* 1, 73, preferred to render, "and Noah, since there was not a righteous man in his generation, found grace and mercy and mercy . . ." He defended this as more probable than "since he was not just."

32. *GenR* 30.9.

so punish was painful to the LORD, the LORD finds no pleasure in the death of anyone who dies, only that they repent and live (see Ezek 18:32). Or, they were the seven days of mourning for the righteous Methuselah, who died in the six hundredth year of Noah, that is, the year of the flood (*Targum Ps-Jonathan, Rashi*).

The generation of the flood was neither warned nor given time for repentance? The baptismal homily of 1 Pet 3:20 allowed them time for repentance: "God patiently waited in the days of Noah during the building of the ark." *1 Clement* 7:6 records that Noah preached repentance, and those who obeyed were saved. *Targum Ps-Jonathan* postulates that the seven days before the flood were given the world to repent and be forgiven.

> ### MATTHEW 24:37–39
> For as it was in the days of Noah, so will it be at the coming of the Son of Man. In those days before the flood, they were eating and drinking, marrying and giving in marriage, up to the day that Noah entered the ark. They did not know until the flood came and carried them all away. So will it be at the coming of the Son of Man.

The physicality in *"the Lord shut him in"* (Gen 7:16) provoked comments. The Targums are one in speaking of the Lord protecting Noah. Rashi elaborates: so that they could not smash up the ark, "they" referring to the giants and the generation of the flood trying to frustrate God's plans. In fact, Wis 14:6 says that the giants were those destroyed in the flood: "For of old, when the proud giants were being destroyed, the hope of the universe, who took refuge on a raft, left to the world a future for the human family, under the guidance of your hand."

In Christian tradition, the ark is a figure of the church saved by the wood on which there hung the Mediator between God and men, himself man, Jesus Christ.[33] The flood waters symbolize the waters of Baptism in which God washes away the sin of the world. 1 Peter 3:20–21 tells the neophytes that the salvation of eight persons in the ark prefigures Baptism which saves them. In formula A of the Blessing and Invocation of God over Baptismal Water, the priest prays, among other things: "The waters of the great Flood you made a sign of the waters of baptism, that make an end of

---

33. Augustine, *City of God*, 15.26, in ACCS, 131.

sin and a new beginning of goodness." The flood became also a symbol of how sudden the coming of the Son of Man will be.

In the Greek context, Plato and Philo hold the world eternal and indestructible.[34] The writer of 2 Pet 3:6–7, 12 however recalls that the world was destroyed by deluge and affirms that the present heavens and earth have been reserved for fire; the heavens will be dissolved in flames and the elements melted by fire. In the analogy of the flood, the waters destroyed life on earth, not the earth itself.[35] So does this text move towards a smelting process in which the wicked are smelted away, hence transformation, not destruction. Adams,[36] after a thorough study, rejects the claim of transformation, not destruction. The scenario involves the destruction of the earth along with the material heavens. However, for him the thought of the creator "recycling" the old to produce the new has positive environmental resonances.

34. Plato, *Timaeus* 32–33; Philo, *On the Eternity of the World*.

35. Kreider, "Flood as Bad as It Gets," 434.

36. Adams, "Retrieving the Earth from the Conflagration," 118.

CHAPTER 7

Genesis 9

Blessing and Covenant; Noah Plants a Vineyard

How could I give you up, Ephraim, or deliver you up, Israel? . . . My heart is overwhelmed, my pity is stirred. I will not give vent to my blazing anger, I will not destroy Ephraim again: for I am God and not a man.

—HOSEA 11:8, 9

In Genesis 8, the Lord undertook "never again" to engage in uncreation activity, the type of the flood. Now, God recreates a new world, with adjustments in view of what has transpired. Genesis 9:1–7 forms an inclusio framed by the theme of *increase and multiply*. The language harks back to Genesis 1: Noah is the new Adam who receives the same blessing to increase, and multiply, and fill the earth.

The Blessing

To Noah and his sons God renews the blessing of Gen 1:28: *be fertile and multiply and fill the earth*. God raises human beings above the animal world even further than before. In Gen 1:28 humans are to subdue (*kabash*) the earth and have dominion (*radah*) over all living things in it. The verbs *kabash* and *radah* indeed belong to the language of conquest, but what about the resistance? If the earth was full of violence (Gen 6:11), surely the animal world participated in such lawlessness? So, God strikes the whole animal world (beasts of earth, birds of the air, fishes of the sea) with *fear and dread* of humankind, delivering them into their power. God recalls that he gave the green plants for food to humans and all living things (*as I did the green plants*, Gen 1:29). But in the renewed order, *any living creature that moves about shall be yours to eat*. Humans may now kill animals, birds, and fish for food. There is one restriction: they may not eat meat with its lifeblood still in it. All life (*nephesh*) belongs to God. Furthermore, just as the LORD God clothed the man and the woman (Gen 3:21), thereby introducing an element of culture, so also humans may not rend their meat from living beings, as beasts do. Lev 17:11 pushes this further into the prohibition of consuming blood, for *the life (nephesh) of the flesh is in the blood and I have given it to you to make atonement on the altar*. Humans may kill for food, but no one may kill a human being. The Decalogue says sharply: "you shall not kill" (Exod 20:13). That the first command to be given to the postdiluvians is a ban on bloodshed suggests that murder was the endemic vice of the antediluvians.[1] For every human life, God himself stands surety: *I will demand an accounting* (repeated thrice). Even a beast that takes human life is liable to God: *from every animal I will demand it.*[2] God makes himself the *gōᵉl*, the defender, guarantor, and avenger of human life! Then, in a surprising move, God delegates to humankind his commitment as *gōᵉl* of human life,[3] which in effect calls for each one to be keeper of his brother, also for human institutions to administer justice:

> Anyone who sheds the blood of a human being,
> By[4] a human being shall that one's blood be shed.

Every human life is sacred and always to be safeguarded. The traditions will spell out the "how" in various ways (see later). The reason for the inviolability of all human life: *for in the image of God have human beings been made*. In Gen 1:27, the image of God functioned to make human beings representatives of God, wielding dominion over the other beings on earth. Here it functions to preserve and protect all human beings, irrespective of race, color, ability, or other qualities people may or may not possess. Noteworthy is that the human being so protected by God is the very one the desires of

---

1. Alter, *Genesis*, 38.

2. Exod 21: "When an ox gores a man or a woman to death, the ox must be stoned; its meat may be eaten."

3. Bonino, "Covenant of Life," 344.

4. *Ba-adam* can also mean "on account of that human being," or "in compensation for that human being."

whose heart remain evil from youth (Gen 8:21)! God finally repeats the blessing to *be fertile, then, and multiply; abound on earth and subdue[5] it.* Genesis 10 will show this blessing as achieving its goal.

A Covenant

> ### WISDOM 11:23–12:1
> But you have mercy on all, because you can do all things; and you overlook sins for the sake of repentance. For you love all things that are and loathe nothing that you have made; for you would not fashion what you hate. How could a thing remain, unless you willed it; or be preserved, had it not been called forth by you? But you spare all things, because they are yours, O Ruler and Lover of souls, for your imperishable spirit is in all things.

The next section, Gen 9:8–17, revolves around the theme of covenant; there are many repetitions. The language of "covenant" with a "sign" has its closest parallel in Genesis 17 (covenant with Abraham). God's gracious commitment to Abraham has a counterpart in God's gracious commitment to humanity as a whole.[6] "Having rescued the righteous remnant from the lethal waters, God now makes a covenant with them, just as he will with the people Israel at Sinai after enabling them to escape across the Sea of Reeds (Exod chs 14–15; 19)."[7] "Covenant" here, as in Genesis 17, is a steadfast and unconditioned promise of God. The "never again" of Gen 8:21 is now formalized in an undertaking by God with every human being and every living creature *for all ages to come.* God promises that *there shall not be another flood to devastate the earth.* And as a sign of the commitment, *I will set my bow in the clouds to serve as a sign of the covenant between me and the earth.* When the bow appears in the clouds, *I will remember my covenant between me and you and every living creature.* All flesh and the earth itself[8] are now valued in a way that was not the case before the flood; the covenant is as much with them as with humankind. The bow is a weapon of war that does not feature in any of the ancient myths of the flood. Rather

---

5. The text repeats *rebū*, multiply, as in the first half of the phrase, but many versions replace this with *redū*, subdue, as in the parallel, Gen 1:28.

6. Scholars attribute both passages to the Priestly Writer.

7. *Jewish Study Bible*, 24.

8. Habel, *Ecological Commentary on Genesis 1–11*, 109.

in the *Enuma Elish* account of creation, Marduk hung his no longer needed bow in the sky. YHWH's use of bow and arrows as weapons is amply demonstrated in the Bible, for example, Hab 3:9; Ps 18:15. Here, however, the bow serves only as sign of the divine graciousness.

Noah Plants a Vineyard. The Curse of Ham

In a second historical notice (the first was in Gen 6:10), the narrator informs us of the sons of Noah, Shem, Ham, and Japheth, adding that *from them the whole earth was populated.* The verb *naphaṣ* really means "to scatter." Its use here points to conscious linkage with Gen 11:9, "from there the Lord scattered [verb, *naphaṣ*] them over all the earth."[9] The narrator gives Ham the epithet, *father of Canaan* in vv. 18 and 22. This is an authorized gloss to aid the proper understanding of the text,[10] or a redactional addition to link with the group of brothers in the Table of Nations (particularly, Gen 10:6).[11] From here on, individual characters often represent political entities as well as family members.[12] Shem, Ham, and Japheth have become eponymous ancestors who represent diverse peoples.

Noah became a tiller of the soil and was the first to plant a vineyard. The curse-free earth is fully alive again. In planting a vineyard, Noah fulfills his father Lamech's prophecy at his birth that *this one shall bring us relief from our work and the toil of our hands . . .* (Gen 5:29). Literally, it says, "this one shall comfort us," as wine gladdens the heart of man (Ps 104:15). It is possible that the author insists (as before for elements of human culture in Gen 4) that the cultivation of vines and the invention of wine making were human inventions and did not come from some god or other as in the myths of surrounding peoples (for example, the myth of Dionysius and wine making among the Greeks).[13]

Noah drank some of the wine, became drunk, and lay naked inside his tent. *Ham, the father of Canaan, saw his father's nakedness, and he told his*

---

9. Cf. Cassuto, *From Noah to Abraham*, 141. He thus argues that the section runs from Gen 9:18 to 11:9.

10. Weingreen, *From Bible to Mishnah*, 34, 48. What Ham did foreshadowed the behavior of Canaan. In short, Canaan was not cursed for the sin of Ham, rather belief in the accursed situation of Canaan is given a foundation in the behavior of the ancestor.

11. Zobel, "*Kena'an*," 216.

12. Mann, *Book of the Torah*, 25.

13. Cassuto, *From Noah to Abraham*, 157.

two brothers outside. They got hold of a robe, walked backward, and covered their father without seeing his nakedness. Noah woke from his wine and learned what his youngest son had done to him. Why now speak of Ham as the youngest son? The Jewish commentator, Ibn Ezra (1089–1164), thought that the original victim was Ham, whose youngest son was Canaan.[14] And why say, *what he had done to him*? Various traditions (see below) make Ham do something dastardly to his father Noah. I agree with Cassuto that if the covering of the nakedness of their father was an adequate remedy, it follows that the misdemeanor was confined to seeing.[15] Noah cursed Canaan: *Cursed be Canaan! The lowest of slaves shall he be to his brothers.* Ham sins and Canaan is cursed? *The New Jerusalem Bible* tried to explain:

> Ham is not mentioned again and Canaan is the one to be cursed in vv. 25–27, so he was evidently the guilty party. His name stood alone in the original narrative set down by the Yahwist, as being the youngest of Noah's three sons, the order of whom, according to this tradition, was therefore Shem, Japheth, and Canaan.

This repeats the view of Wellhausen that the youngest son of Noah was indeed Canaan. The problem is that the text says clearly that Ham, not Canaan, was the perpetrator. Some say that Ham could not be cursed because he was already blessed by God (Gen 9:1). Or it may be that, as in the older tradition of the Hebrew Bible, it was considered just to punish parents with their entire families or in their children until the third and fourth generation (Exod 34:7). However, this met with opposition around the time of the Babylonian exile. People complained that "parents eat sour grapes, but the children's teeth are set on edge" (Ezek 18:2). The LORD's answer was, "all life belongs to me; the father's life and the son's life, both alike belong to me. The one who has sinned is the one to die" (Ezek 18:4; cf. Jer 31:29–30). Accordingly, when the divine attributes of Exod 34:7 came to be repeated in Deut 7:9–10, they read that Yahweh "punishes *in their own persons* those that hate him. He destroys anyone who hates him, without delay; and it is *in their own persons* that he punishes them" (italics mine). Deuteronomy 24:16 legislates that "parents may not be put to death for their children, nor children for parents, but each must be put to death for his own crime."

---

14. See Speiser, *Genesis*, 62.

15. Cassuto, *From Noah to Abraham*, 151.

Many exegetes who view the curse on the politico-ethnic level say that the Israelites (sons of Shem) and the Philistines (sons of Japheth) did in fact subjugate the Canaanites (sons of Ham).

> The Canaanites were to suffer the curse and the bondage not because of the sins of Ham, but because they themselves acted like him, because of their own transgressions which resembled those attributed to him in this allegory.[16]

Cassuto believes that "let Canaan be his slave" refers to the enslaving of four Canaanite cities under Chedorlaomer (Gen 14).[17] *'Ebed* (servant, slave) being a technical term for political subordination, the theme of Gen 9:25 is to express the total subjection and subservience of the Canaanites.[18]

But who or what was Canaan? In the Amarna Letters, the term *Canaan* is a political designation for the third Egyptian province whose capital was Gaza. In much of the Hebrew Bible, though boundaries and relationships shifted, the term denoted both a territory and the pre-Israelite population of Palestine.[19] In Gen 10:6, Canaan[20] was the fourth son of Ham, the others being Cush, Mizraim (Egypt), and Put (Libya?). Cush usually refers to Ethiopia, but the reference here must be other, for Cush's son, Nimrod, established a kingdom in Babylon, Erech, and Akkad (10:8–10).

It is a consistent tradition in the Torah that the Canaanites' loss of their land is punishment for guilt. Genesis 15:14 speaks of the iniquity of the Amorites (whom the Elohist calls "Amorites," the Yahwist calls "Canaanites") reaching its full extent; Deut 9:5 says that

> it is not because of your justice or the integrity of your heart that you are going in to take possession of their land, but it is because of their wickedness that the Lord, your God, is dispossessing these nations before you and in order to fulfill the promise he made on oath to your ancestors.

16. Ibid., 155.

17. Ibid., 168. The descendants of Canaan inhabited Sodom, Gomorrah, Admah, and Zeboiim (Gen 10:19). These cities noted for sodomy and inhospitality in Gen 13 and destroyed in Gen 19. These were the four cities that served (*'abedū*, were in slavery to) Chedorlaomer, king of Elam (Gen 14), who in Gen 10:22 is the first son of Shem.

18. Zobel, "*Kena'an*," 216.

19. Ibid., 217, citing Noth, *Old Testament World*, 53–54.

20. The descendants of Canaan were Sidon, Heth, also the Jebusites, Amorites, Girgashites, Hivites, Arkites, Sinites, Arvadites, Zemarites, and the Hamathites (10:15–18). The Canaanite borders were from Sidon all the way to Gerar, near Gaza, and all the way to Sodom, Gomorrah, Admah, and Zeboiim, near Lasha (Gen 10:19).

"Canaanite" became a code name for sexual perversion and for peoples to be uprooted from their land. Warrior, a Native American, views the plight of Native Americans through the prism of the biblical Canaanites, as people who have no identity, simply peoples whom the LORD removes in order to install the sons of Israel.[21]

Genesis 9:18–27 has been misused by powerful kingdoms and nations through time, a misuse that unmasks the ethical irresponsibility of countless generations of exegetes. From early times, this text became a foundational text that authorized the enslaving of dark-skinned people. Ham was turned into a dark-skinned person through linguistic maneuver.[22] The Apartheid System in South Africa availed of Gen 9:18–27 with Josh 9:27 (Joshua decreed that the Gibeonites should forever be hewers of wood and drawers of water) to justify both the reservation of jobs for whites and oppressive policies against the indigenous African population.[23] On the strength of the "curse of Ham," Islamic Arabs for centuries raided the East African coast for slaves. Since the fifteenth century, Europeans have found in the "curse of Ham" the key justification for the enslavement of colored peoples. The American slave trade in addition associated the curse of Ham with the theory of the racial inferiority of black peoples.[24]

What does it say that the curse constitutes the first words we hear from Noah and is the only humanly-imposed curse in the Torah![25] Much has been written about the magic power of words in the ancient Near East, especially when spoken by the aged and people in certain positions. The curse is said to be a word of power that follows the accursed: "the dissolution which takes place in the soul of the sinner . . . as a poisonous, consuming substance that destroys and undermines, so that the soul falls to pieces and its strength is exhausted."[26] In short, the curse dries up the springs of life generated by blessing. In more traditional societies, fear of the power of the curse, especially by an acknowledged righteous person or respected elder, is a potent moral deterrent. However, although Scripture contains

21. Cf. Warrior, "Native American Perspective," 277–85.

22. The name Ham derives from the Hebrew root *hūm*, which refers to heat, warmness, and by extension to people in warm climates. See Copher, "Three Thousand Years," 105–28; Felder, "Race, Racism and the Biblical Narratives," 127–45.

23. Cf. Wittenberg, "Let Canaan Be His Slave," 46–56.

24. Bradley, "Curse of Canaan and the American Negro," 109.

25. Goldingay, *Israel's Gospel*, 184.

26. Pedersen, *Israel: Its Life and Culture*, 2:437.

cases in which a blessing or curse once uttered cannot be taken back (think of Isaac's wrong blessing of Jacob in Gen 27), its overall point of view is that a person's word cannot coerce God or have the power to effect what it says without God's will. Cassuto notes that the verbs used in Hebrew appear mostly in the jussive, that is, in the grammatical form that expresses request or prayer.[27]

We have by now seen enough of the family to realize it is a troubled and troubling place![28] Husband-wife relationships soured in Adam and Eve, a brother killed another, and now a father curses and condemns one of his three sons to enslavement. Florence reflects on the moral dilemmas when there is an elephant in the family room.[29] Ham is the character for whom preserving life means naming what you see, calling it by name. His brothers understand preserving life as protecting family honor. Noah understands preserving life in the language of proscription, casting out a third of his family. What is the right thing to do is not always clear in some circumstances.

Blessed be the Lord, the God of Shem! Let Canaan be his slave. May God expand Japheth, and may he dwell among the tents of Shem, and let Canaan be his slave. The general name for deity, Elohim, is used for Japheth as one outside of Israel. The blessing puns on the name Japheth: *yapht* (may expand) Japheth. Genesis 10:2 gives the descendants of Japheth as Gomer, Magog, Madak, Javan (Greece), Tubal, Meshech and Tiras—generally the Indo-European groups to the north and west. Some of these settled along the coastline of Palestine as Philistines.

> Philistine possession of part of the promised land, which belonged by rights to the people of Yahweh, was explained as the result of Noah's prayer that God would give a broad territory to the ancestor of the Philistines, so that he might even dwell in the tents of Shem; the presence of the Philistines in Canaan is thus ultimately ascribed to God himself.[30]

A clue to the possible timing of the blessing is that the Philistines seem absorbed within Israel. In the time of the Judges and under Saul and David, the Philistines were a hostile power that fought continually with Israel. Speiser notes that in Gen 10:14 the Philistines had ceased to be a

27. Cassuto, *Commentary on the Book of Genesis*, 2:156.

28. Goldingay, *Israel's Gospel*, 185.

29. Florence, "After the Flood," 43.

30. Zobel, "*Kena'an*," 222.

politically significant group and were settled long enough to be classed with the Hamites,[31] not the Japhites.

Tradition

In blessing Noah and his sons, God blessed all of humanity. This blessing contained two prohibitions: that of murder and of eating meat with its lifeblood still in it. These two formed the nucleus of what came to be known as the Seven Noachide Laws, that is, laws incumbent on the whole of humanity.

The first listing of the Noachide Laws was in the Tosephta, with final sanction in the Talmud (b. Sanh 56a):

> Our Rabbis taught: seven precepts were the sons of Noah commanded: social laws; to refrain from blasphemy, idolatry; adultery; bloodshed; robbery; and eating flesh cut from a living animal.

"Social laws" is interpreted as establishing courts of justice or observing social justice. That something like this tradition was in place before the Christian era can be seen in the decision of the Council of Jerusalem in Acts 15. To foster relationships and commensality between Christian Jews and Gentiles, the Council prescribed that Christian Gentiles abstain from meat sacrificed to idols, from blood, from meats of strangled animals and from unlawful marriage (Act 15:29). Draining the blood is the origin of kashering, the Jewish practice of salting meat to absorb the blood before cooking.[32]

For murder, Num 35:30 envisages a court process: "Whenever someone kills another, the evidence of witnesses is required to kill the murderer. A single witness does not suffice for putting a person to death." And what if there are no witnesses? *Targum Ps-Jonathan* specifies that in such case the Lord of the world will take revenge of him on the day of the great judgment. Genesis 9:5 was also interpreted as prohibiting suicide: "And surely your blood of your lives will I require" (Gen 9:5). R. Eleazar (end of first century CE) remarked that it meant "I will require your blood if shed by the hands of yourselves, for murder is perhaps different" (b. Baba Kamma 91b). From Gen 9:6, the rabbis derived the prohibition of abortion: "On the authority of R. Ishmael (90–135 CE) it was said: [He is executed] even for the murder

31. Speiser, *Genesis*, 63.
32. *Jewish Study Bible*, 25.

of an embryo. What is R. Ishmael's reason? Because it is written, Whoso sheddeth the blood of man within [another] man,[33] shall his blood be shed. What is a man within another man?—An embryo in his mother's womb" (b. Sanh 57b).

Recent Catholic teaching gives a nuanced perspective on the death penalty. On the one hand, "Legitimate public authority has the right and duty to inflict punishment proportionate to the gravity of the offense. Punishment has the primary aim of redressing the disorder introduced by the offense" (*Catechism of the Catholic Church*, #2266). As far as possible, it must contribute to the correction of the guilty party. "The traditional teaching of the Church does not exclude recourse to the death penalty, if this is the only possible way of effectively defending human lives against the unjust aggressor" (#2267). On the other hand, it is more in keeping with the common good and the dignity of the human person for the authority to limit itself to nonlethal means if these are sufficient to defend and protect people's safety from the aggressor. Today, "in fact, the cases in which the execution of the offender is an absolute necessity are very rare, if not practically nonexistent" (ibid.), for the state has many possibilities for effectively preventing crime without definitely taking away the possibility of one redeeming himself (nos. 2266–2267 need be read in their entirety).

The Natural Moral Law is a counterpart of the Noachide Laws. The *Catechism of the Catholic Church* teaches as follows.

CATECHISM #1955

The natural law is written and engraved in the soul of each and every man, because it is human reason ordaining him to do good and forbidding him to sin . . . But this command of human reason would not have the force of law if it were not the voice and interpreter of a higher reason to which our spirit and our freedom must be submitted (#1954). The "divine and natural" law shows man the way to follow so as to practice the good and attain his end

---

Why call Ham *his youngest [qaṭan] son*? Because he was little in merit.[34] He proved his worthlessness by telling his brothers such sensitive

---

33. Instead of reading *ba-adam* as by a human being, this reading moves the pause to after *ba-adam*: anyone who sheds the blood of a human being in a human, his blood will be shed.

34. *Tg Pseudo-Jonathan.*

news in public: in the marketplace (*Neofiti* 1), in the street (*Onqelos* and *Pseudo-Jonathan*). *Noah woke up from his wine and learned what his youngest son had done to him*. Some rabbis thought of some act like castration. Rabbi Berekiah (fourth century): you have prevented me from begetting a young son to serve me, therefore that man (your son) will be a servant to his brethren.[35] Ham sinned and Canaan is cursed? Rabbi Nehemiah (mid-second century): it was Canaan who saw it and informed them.[36] Ephrem the Syrian[37] took up this reasoning. Ham was the middle son and not the youngest. Many therefore say it was Canaan, the youngest, who told of Noah's nakedness, then Ham went out and *jokingly* told his brothers (italics mine). Canaan was thus justly cursed, for he was not cursed in the place of another. Noah knew that Canaan in his old age would deserve the curse.

35. *GenR* 36.7.

36. Ibid.

37. *Commentary on Genesis*, 7.3.1–2, in ACCS, 158.

CHAPTER 8

Genesis 10–11

Table of Nations; Dispersion over the Face of the Earth

> *What are human beings, that you make much of them,*
> *or pay them any heed?*
>
> —JOB 7:17

Introduction to Genesis 10

Genesis 10 shows how effective the new blessing on humankind has been: *from these* [the three sons of Noah] *the nations of the earth branched out after the flood* (Gen 10:32). "Chapter 10 tells us that human beings spread over the earth; 11:1–9 tell us why."[1] In fact, Genesis 10 takes the division of languages for granted. The colophon to each of the three sections speaks of descendants of the sons of Noah distinguished *by their lands, each with its own language, according to their clans, by their nations* (vv. 5, 20, 31). Genesis 10:18 (families of Canaanites) uses the same root, *phuṣ* (to scatter), linking with Gen 11:9 where the same root appears when the Lord scattered the generation of the tower.

The classification of the peoples is not uniform, nor is it merely ethno-linguistic. There are names of individuals, plural nouns representing tribes, gentilic names, and place names. "Son of" and "begot" formulas often designate figurative relationships, not ones of blood. It is clear that several criteria have been used: anthropological, linguistic, political, and

---

1. Mann, *Book of the Torah*, 25.

geographical.[2] This sometimes led to confusion. For example, Cush is son of Ham (v. 7), yet is father of Nimrod who established kingdoms in Mesopotamia, the region of the sons of Shem (vv. 8–12). Sheba and Havilah are both sons of Cush, in the line of Ham (v. 7) and sons of Joktan, line of Shem (vv. 28, 29). The Philistines (v. 14) ethnically belong to the tribes of Japhet, but are classed among the Hamites (see below).

Two elements of structure betray the function of the genealogy. The order of sons is inverted to end with Shem, explicitly designated as *the ancestor of all the children of Eber* (v. 21). Eber is the eponymous ancestor of the Hebrews about whom the entire story is told. A second signal: "More attention is given to the line of Ham than to that of Japheth or Shem."[3] The point is driven home in v. 19: *so that the Canaanite borders extended from Sidon all the way to Gerar, near Gaza, and all the way to Sodom, Gomorrah, Admah and Zeboiim, near Lasha.* These were the wider boundaries of the promised land (see Gen 15:18; Deut 11:24; 1 Kgs 8:25; 2 Kgs 14:25) and conform to those of the Egyptian Province called Canaan, which also commenced with Sidon. Japhethites are roughly to the north, the sons of Shem to the east and south. In this classification, Israel already circumscribes the land of Canaan which will become her homeland[4] and shows the geographical and political relations of this land to its neighbors. All the while, Israel shows that the divine intention to fill the earth has been achieved in the distribution of the nations over the face of the earth.[5] The total number of nations is seventy (not counting Noah and his sons and counting Sidon once), which is the number of the sons of God (Deut 32:8; variant: sons of Israel) and of the sons of Israel who went down to Egypt (Exod 1:5). The ideology of land in this chapter is that of a host country, similar to the ideology of land in the Abraham story. Peoples, cultures, and nations expand across earth without conflict or subordinating other peoples.[6] "All these peoples apparently have a right to their domains."[7]

---

2. Ross, "Table of Nations in Genesis 10: Structure," 348.

3. Ross, "Table of Nations in Genesis 10—Its Content," 24.

4. Ross, "Table of Nations—Content," 30: "That the promised land is central to the Table can be seen from the arrangement of the descendants. Moreover, the preoccupation with the Canaanites in the land of promise shows the concern of the writer."

5. Cf. Cassuto, *Commentary on the Book of Genesis*, 2:172.

6. See Habel, *Ecological Reading of Genesis 1–11*, 121.

7. Ibid., 122.

The Sons of Japheth

These are generally the Indo-European peoples to the north. Jawan is Greece. Speiser thinks that Tarshish should be sought in the Island of Rhodes, though he admits that the usual practice is to adduce Greek Tartessos (in Spain).[8] The Hebrew text has Dodanim (v. 4), but most versions read Rodanim (people of island of Rhodes) with 1 Chron 1:7.[9]

The Sons of Ham

Speiser speaks of the use of Cush for two widely separated lands—for Ethiopia (as he thinks is here the case) and the country of the Kassites (as in v. 8 and Gen 2:13).[10] Cassuto finds it difficult to identify Cush here with either. He prefers to identify it with the west semitic tribes called *Kwšw* in the Egyptian Execration Texts of the second half of the nineteenth century BCE. These lived south of Israel or the Transjordan and were in the course of time absorbed among the Midianites.[11] The combination of Cush and Havilah appears also in Gen 2:13. The case of Nimrod has been mentioned above. Many scholars believe Nimrod's exploits reflect those of Tukulti-Ninurta 1 (thirteenth century BCE), the first Assyrian conqueror of Babylonia. "Ninurta's acts of heroism as a warrior and hunter were portrayed in Mesopotamian mythology as preceding his founding of Mesopotamian civilization, and he was regarded as king of the universe."[12] The report that Nimrod *was a mighty hunter in the eyes of YHWH* (v. 8), using the confessional name of Israel's God, is puzzling. Does this indicate divine approval of Nimrod's exploits? And how does the apparently positive mention of Babylon here relate to the swipe at Babel in Gen 11:9? Some late Jewish midrashim (see at Gen 11:9) turn Nimrod into a rebel against YHWH, even the one who incited the building of the tower. There are textual variants at v. 11. The Hebrew text says that *from that land he* [Nimrod] *went forth to Assyria, where he built Nineveh . . .* Augustine already remarked that Assur, father of the Assyrians, was not one of the sons of Ham, but is found among

---

8. Speiser, *Genesis*, 66.

9. Though the *Qere* (instruction for what is to be read, as distinguished from what is written) at 1 Chron 1:7 reverts to Dodanim!

10. Speiser, *Genesis*, 66.

11. Cassuto, *Commentary on the Book of Genesis*, 2:198.

12. Smith, "What Hope after Babel?," 188n22.

the sons of Shem (v. 22).[13] Speiser is among scholars who render: *From that land came Asshur. And he built Nineveh . . .* There are also variants at v. 14 for the origin of the Philistines. The Hebrew text has: *the Casluhim—whence the Philistines came forth—and the Caphtorim.* The problem with this is that elsewhere in the Hebrew Bible (Deut 2:23; Amos 9:7; Jer 47:4), the origin of the Philistines is given as Caphtor (Crete). Most modern versions thus invert the order to render: *the Casluhim, and the Caphtorim from whom the Philistines came.* As to the association of the Philistines with Egypt, we know that they invaded Egypt in the time of Rameses III (beginning of the twelfth century BCE), were beaten back, but allowed to settle on the Canaanite coast.[14] It is significant, as Habel points out, that throughout the genealogy of Ham Canaan is not cursed, only portrayed as ancestor whose progeny spreads across particular domains of earth. It is a host country to several peoples and "there is no hint of pollution by false deities or other impediments."[15]

The Sons of Shem

Right at the beginning (v. 21) it is noted that Shem is the father of Eber (see above). To this, Augustine countered that Shem did not beget Eber, who was indeed in the fifth generation from him. Why then the link here? The Hebrews, whose story this is, derived their name from Eber.[16] The genealogy of Shem will be picked up and treated at greater length in Gen 11:10–26; there also more will be said about Peleg. For now, it is only mentioned that in his time the world was divided (root *palag* puns on name Peleg). Is this a reference forward to the Babel incident? Fouts, comparing the meaning of canal for Akkadian *palgu* and Ugaritic *plg*, suggests the possibility that in Peleg's time occurred the widespread canalization of the land of Mesopotamia.[17]

---

13. *City of God*, 16.3, in ACCS, 162.

14. See Cassuto, *Commentary on the Book of Genesis*, 2:207–8, for Cassuto's student Y. M. Grintz's proposal of three successive waves of Philistine immigration, the earliest of which from Casluhim in Egypt.

15. Habel, *Ecological Reading of Genesis 1–11*, 121.

16. *City of God*, 16.3, in ACCS, 162.

17. Fouts, "Peleg in Gen 10:25," 20.

Introduction to Genesis 11

Genesis 11:1–9 is a narrative that interrupts a genealogy, just as the narrative on Nimrod (Gen 10:8–12) interrupts a genealogy.[18] It is intriguing that both units are about Babel (10:10; 11:9). Some traditions and interpreters seek to interpret them in reference to each other. Most standard versions headline the unit of Gen 11:1–9 as "The Tower of Babel"; *The New African Bible* has "Temptation of the Totalitarian Power," again focusing on the tower. However, exegetes are perplexed about how to read this unit. Part of the problem is uncertainty as to the locus of the evil or sin, if any. At least four suggestions have appeared. When one focuses on "they stopped building the city" (v. 8), it looks as if city culture itself is being portrayed as alienation from God. A tower with its top reaching the heavens is often seen as symbol of insolent rebellion and the effort to cross forbidden boundaries: "a physical link between the divine and human realms."[19] Third, focusing on the human proposal, *otherwise we shall be scattered all over the earth* (v. 4), and the divine counter that "scattered them from there over all the earth" (v. 8, using the same verbal root, *pûṣ*), it looks as if the evil was in a conscious transgression of the divine command to fill the earth and subdue it. Finally, there is the quest for a name and the fact that YHWH gratuitously purposed to make Abram's name great (Gen 12:2). Was the evil then one of self-exaltation and vainglory?

Genesis 11:10 picks up the genealogy of Shem from Gen 10:21–31, with Peleg and his line, dropping the line of Joktan, mainly Arabic peoples. Genesis 10:21 announced in advance that Shem was "ancestor of all the children of Eber." *'Eber* is the same root as *'Ibri* (Hebrew) that designates both a people and a language. From Eber through Peleg comes Abram on whom the story will focus.

Genesis 11:1–9

We implied above that narrative criticism is not monolithic, but may vary according to where the reader places the focus. Before giving three interpretations of this unit, I look at the unit's structure and the crafted language and outline areas of note and some of general agreement. The structure is clearly bipartite and highlights reversal. The clash of the human and divine

18. Source critics speak of Yahwist narrative and Priestly genealogy.

19. Mann, *Book of Torah*, 26.

projects is clear even in the use of language. "Come, let us . . . otherwise we shall be scattered all over the earth" (v. 4) clashes with "come, let us go down and confuse their language . . . so the Lord scattered them from there" (vv. 7, 8). Fokkelman sets up the Hebrew text as a chiasm with the turning point in v. 5, the descent of the Lord (the force is slightly diminished in translation).[20]

The whole world has the same language (v. 1)

There (*sham*, v. 2)

(said) one to another (v. 3)

Come, let us mold bricks (v. 3)

Let us build ourselves (v. 4)

A city and a tower (v. 4)

The Lord came down to see (v. 5)

The city and the tower (v. 5)

That the people had built (v. 5)

Come, let us go down (v. 7)

One the language of another (v. 7)

From there (*mi–sham*, v. 8)

Confused the speech of all the earth (v. 9).

There may or not may not be satire in saying that "they used bricks for stone, and bitumen for mortar" (v. 3). The narrator may have simply reflected the Mesopotamian context of alluvial soil, different from Canaan where stone is abundant. But, there may be satire when it is said that YHWH came down to see the city and tower that "the sons of *adam*" have built. Some approaches find the satire in YHWH coming down to inspect the tower supposed to reach to heaven. But there is satire when the builders are called "sons of *adam*" (*bene ha-adam*; unfortunately NABRE dissimulates in rendering, *that the people had built*). Used as a common name, *adam* signifies humanity. When used in binary contrast to divinity, it implies limitation, the "not-god" aspect. Some interpreters find satire in the etiology of Babel based on the partial verbal clang of Babel and *balal* (v. 9): *that is why it was called Babel, because there the LORD confused the speech of all the world.* As Ross put it, "because YHWH 'made a babble' their language."[21] For some, Babel thus means "Confusion." But *balal* literally means "to mix" (for ex-

20. Fokkelman, *Narrative Art in Genesis*, 22.

21. Ross, "Dispersion of the Nations," 122.

ample, ingredients for sacrifices), hence the translation should be: "there YHWH mixed their speech," initiating a world of differentiated languages in place of the one language they started with.[22] YHWH's speech in v. 6 is difficult to interpret: *If now, while they are one people and all have the same language, they have started to do this, nothing they presume to do will be out of their reach.* In few occasions, *hen/hinneh* can be translated by "if"; however, in this case, Hiebert[23] may be right that the demonstrative *hen* (behold) points to what is there before the eyes: there is one people and they have one language. But what is motivating YHWH? Is it the motif of "breaking the bounds"[24] which is said to recur in the primeval history, humanity all the time straining to break out into the divine realm and God reasserting the boundary between human and divine? The various interpretations of this unit handle this verse in different ways. In one of these, rather than the musings of a jealous God, we encounter the resolve for a necessary course correction ultimately beneficial to humans. The etiology of Babel in v. 9 is puzzling. The story started with the whole of humanity "there"; does Babel here still stand for all humanity, or the historical kingdom of Babylon? Is there satire and irony here? There now follow three illustrative interpretations of the unit.

ZEPHANIAH 3:9–10

For then I make pure the speech of the peoples, that they may all call upon the name of the LORD, to serve him with one accord. From beyond the rivers of Ethiopia and as far as the recessed of the North, they shall bring me offerings.

---

1. The Sin Is Hubris, Scattering the Punishment

The common and widespread interpretation is that of sin and punishment. The story of the tower is presented as the climax in a series of sin-punishment-mitigation scenarios that run through Genesis 1–11. It lacks the mitigation element, a function said to be fulfilled by the story of Abram.

---

22. Hiebert, "Tower of Babel," 47.

23. Ibid., 43–44.

24. Clines, "Significance of the 'Sons of God' Episode," 36.

The entire unit is read as satire upon Babylon and her megalomaniac pretenses. The central focus is on the tower. *The whole world had the same language.* This is to be expected of people descended from a common ancestor. However, it is not in sync with Genesis 10 where the refrain has people already classified "according to their clans, according to their languages, by their lands, by their nations" (see 10:31). *In the land of Shinar.* The very same Hebrew expression occurs in 10:10 designating the beginning of the kingdom of Nimrod as Babel, Erech, Accad, and Calneh, in the land of Shinar. The narrator explains to readers of Palestine that the location being alluvial plain, the people could only bake bricks for building. Some see this as satire, especially that "they used bricks for stone, and bitumen for mortar." *Come, let us build ourselves a city and a tower with its top in the sky.* "Sky" in this translation is neutral. Interpreters generally render *bashamayim* as "in the heavens." In a two-tier universe, a tower with its top in the heavens is seen as an attempt to storm heaven, breach God's space. For some, what is envisaged is a ziggurat-type construction, a physical link between earth and heaven. A ziggurat usually has a shrine on top. Ross argues that Gen 11:1–9 is a counterblast and polemic against Babylon as the "world-famous city and tower culture claiming to be the heavenly plan and beginning of creation,"[25] as in *Enuma Elish*, Tablet VI, lines 55–64. He finds three correspondences:

> the making of the tower for the sanctuary of the gods, with Genesis reporting the determination to build the tower and city in rebellion to God; the lofty elevation of its head into the heavens, with Genesis recording almost the same reference; and the making of the bricks before the building of the city, with Genesis describing the process with the same grammatical construction.[26]

And so make a name for ourselves; otherwise we shall be scattered all over the earth. In view of the explicit blessing and command to multiply, fill the earth, and subdue it, Brueggemann comments that this

> attempts to establish a cultural, human oneness without reference to the threats, promises or mandates of God. This is a self-made unity in which humanity has a "fortress mentality." It seeks to survive by its own resources.[27]

25. Ross, "Dispersion of the Nations in Gen 11:1–9," 125.

26. Ibid.

27. Brueggemann, *Genesis*, 99.

Exegetes note that the name they vainly strove for was freely given to Abram in Gen 12:2. Further, the desire for unity is manifestly against the divine command to fill the earth. Hence the generation of the tower set themselves up against God. *The LORD came down to see the city and the tower that [the sons of man] had built.* YHWH had to come down to see the tower which was supposed to storm heaven! All human strivings fall short of the divine. The binary contrast of YHWH and "sons of man" highlights the limited and puny nature of mortal humankind. *If now, while they are one people and all have the same language, they have started to do this, nothing they presume to do will be out of their reach.* This is usually read as a threat of "incipient titanism." It had to be beaten back, as YHWH beat back the effort to rise to divine status through the marriage of the sons of God and daughters of humans (Gen 6:1–4). Smith put it this way: "If the sin is allowed to continue it can only get worse, nothing will be beyond them (cf. Luke 23:31)."[28] Yet YHWH had renounced ever again responding to human acts by the flood. *Come, let us go down and there confuse their language, so that no one will understand the speech of another.* The confusion of language is interpreted as divine punishment and as the immediate cause of the scattering. They feared lest they scatter over the face of the earth; YHWH precisely scattered them over the face of the earth. They therefore stopped building the city, symbol of oneness in vanity. *That is why one calls its name Babel,* that is Confusion, for there YHWH confused the speech of all the world. Proud Babylon that raises itself to the skies is really nothing but confusion and shame. YHWH humbles the proud and arrogant and destroys every human project that gets in the way of the divine project.

2. The Evil Is Imperial Domination

Let the postcolonial reading of Croatto[29] represent this approach. For Croatto, the story was produced by Judeans in exile. It portrays divine action against imperial domination and ridicules the Babylonian foundation myth. The real title should be: "The founding and exile of Babylon." Croatto's method is to bracket out the story as "holy words" and use social analysis in the context of its original production. Croatto outlines three stages of the reading of this text. As etiology for the multiplicity of peoples and tongues, often seen as punishment. Unity of language as tool of imperial

28. Smith, "What Hope after Babel?," 178.
29. Croatto, "Reading of the Story of the Tower of Babel," 203–23.

domination, and diversity of languages as blessing for the oppressed. All humanity concentrated into a political and economic center (the city) is imperial praxis. European colonization points to the suppression of regional and local languages and the abrogation of natural boundaries for borders imposed by the dominant nations. The story is a demand for the freedom of cultures in their twofold ethnic and linguistic dimensions.

The unit opposes unity/one language and diversity/dispersion. The text divides into the following subunits.

- Unity of language and habitat (vv. 1–2);
- The human project: economic and political (vv. 3–4);
- YHWH's appearance (v. 5);
- Yahweh's anti-project (vv. 6–7);
- Dispersion (v. 8); and
- The name of Babylon (v. 9).

It is not clear who the "they" of v. 2 who settled in Shinar are: the inhabitants of the whole earth (v. 1), or a section of the world population? In the latter case, v. 2 would be the beginning of a new section.

Stone is scarce in Mesopotamia, so they made walls of bricks, baked or not. The tower is the ziggurat, a feature of the great cities of Babylon. The ziggurat stood for a mountain and symbolized the abode of the gods. Hence every temple was looked upon as a mountain. The ziggurat has a shrine at the bottom and at the top. The ziggurat of Babylon was called é-temen-an-ki, that is, house of the foundation of heaven and earth. City and tower have the tutelary god of the city and the king as referents. The tower is the fortified sector of the city where the king and his administration reside and where the apparatus of cult is placed, hence the acropolis. The irony is that the tower was supposed to reach heaven, yet YHWH needed to descend to see what they had built. In YHWH's view, they have to be stopped or they will do whatever they wish. This may be the motif of the "envy of the gods" (see Gen 3:22). The story registers divine suspicion regarding human striving for infinity (v. 6). The rivalry between YHWH and the Mesopotamian gods is shown in Ps 78:69: "he built his shrine like the heavens, like the earth, which he founded forever." Jer 51:53 says that "though Babylon scale the heavens and make her strong heights inaccessible, my destroyers shall reach her," an oracle which reads like a response to Gen 11:4.

The city symbolizes the imperial concentration of power. The aim in building it is not defense, but to make a name for themselves, so as not to disperse (versus the command to "fill the earth" in Gen 9:1, 7). Everything they do speaks of concentration of power: the city as imperial center concentrates populations; the one language is the language of empire, the *lingua franca*; the name acquired by the works acts to prevent dispersion. They become an `*am* (one people) with cultural unity through ethnicity, language, and the imposition of a "normative" worldview.

But then the human project meets with the divine anti-project. The clash is signified even linguistically. *Come, let us build ourselves a city and a tower, let us make a name* (v. 4a) and the divine, *Come, let us go down and confuse their language* (v. 7). He came to see what the humans had built, not what they were building—*banū* indicates finished product. The project was enabled through mutual understanding by way of one language; the anti-project aimed to render impossible any such projects by taking away centralization of power through one language and one culture. *If now, . . . they have started to do this.* They already manifest unlimited power/ possibilities. They have to be stopped or they will do whatever they wish. There is a clang on Job 42:2: "I know that you can do all things, and that no purpose of yours can be hindered." YHWH has unlimited power with regard to what he intends. The primary objective of confusing their language is not dispersion, but to render impossible any great projects in the future (all require centralization through the power of one language). The divine antiproject resulted in, *and they ceased building the city* (v. 8b). The completed tower stands and defies the heavens; the city was finished in v. 5b, but the construction of a city is a never-ending project! *That is why* (v. 9) alerts to etiology. YHWH called the city Babel, that is, confusion, it is built by humans at their own initiative. Babylon (*bab ilim*), "the gate of the gods," was chosen by the victorious Marduk as his dwelling and place of assembly of the gods; it was built by the gods. The story is thus a counter-myth and counter-hegemonic. The central theme is human lack of moderation and YHWH's suspicion of human projects. The center is at v. 6 (not v. 5 as often posited)—the story deals with the undoing of possible human superprojects. The verb for scatter, *pūṣ*, is common in the prophets for the scattering of exile. "The story makes the point that the same Babylon that drives the people of Judah into exile and 'disperses' it over the whole face of the empire will, in turn, 'be dispersed' by YHWH. That is the metamessage of the myth."[30]

3. The Origins of Cultural Difference

Hiebert[31] is among those who argue that the story is exclusively about the origins of cultural difference and not about pride and punishment. For Anderson, the dialectic in the Babel story is as follows: "Man strives to maintain unity, God's action effects diversity . . . Man wants to be safe with homogeneity, God welcomes pluralism."[32] The Babel story thus illuminates a theology of pluralism.

The single language was not imposed, rather was the natural result of descent from the one post-flood family. "The aim of the project . . . has nothing to do with extending the reach of empire but just the opposite: staying in one place (v. 4). The story, thus, is not about the suppression of difference between cultures but about the origins of difference itself."[33] There is no suggestion of royal or imperial motivation or action, as in 10:8–12 where Babel is one of Nimrod's royal cities. Here the people exhort one another and act in democratic fashion, seeking dominion over the limitations of their environment.[34] The narrator's primary interest is not in the tower at all. Anyway, the tower is just a feature of the magnificence of the city and has no ominous connotations. The text is ambiguous on what the sin of the builders was. YHWH was worried about what human success might lead to (v. 6, and see Gen 3:22), but no reason is given in the text for his intervention. The dispersion cannot be act of divine punishment, seeing that Genesis 10 already presented the diversity of languages and ethnic groups as fruit of the divine blessing in Gen 9:1, 7. Ibn Ezra commented that "God scattered the people for their own benefit."

The story is a unity, with two halves that respond to each other: the human activity (vv. 1–4) versus the divine activity (vv. 6–9); God's descent to inspect the human project (v. 5) is the midpoint.

---

30. Croatto, "Tower of Babel," 221.

31. Hiebert, "Tower of Babel," 29–58. Similar, though slightly different, is Anderson, "Unity and Diversity in God's Creation," 69–81.

32. Anderson, "Unity and Diversity," 71.

33. Hiebert, "Tower of Babel," 35.

34. Anderson, "Unity and Diversity," 75.

The builders' motive has nothing to do with pride or rebellion, rather "so that we will not be dispersed over the surface of all the earth" (v. 4). Mann expresses this clearly.

> The clearest expression of the purpose of the tower occurs at the end of v. 4: "lest we be scattered abroad upon the face of the whole earth." The word "scatter" occurs three times within the nine verses of the story (vv. 4, 8, 9), each time with "over the face of the whole earth." The emphasis on this motif suggests that the primary motivation for building the tower is not outright rebellion against God (who is never mentioned in the speech), nor an assault against heaven, nor even arrogance. The real reason for the project is fear. The builders are insecure.[35]

We may not take the people's wish to stay together in the Yahwist's story as a transgression of God's command to "fill the earth" in the Priestly tradition (Gen 1:28; 9:1, 7) as many interpreters have done—there is no such command in J.[36] Building a city and a tower and making a name are all simply means to achieve their goal. They desire to stay in one place. The city is symbol of man's creative freedom to rise above the natural environment, a place of security from the powers of chaos that threaten the outside world. Some anxiety and fear of the unknown is portrayed by "lest we be scattered": "fear of geographical dispersion, fear of linguistic and ethnic diversity, fear of differences of race, religion, custom."[37] "A city and tower" means a city crowned by a tower; the tower is only an aspect of the city. Thus in v. 8, the city is mentioned alone, *and they stopped building the city. Migdal* is used consistently for the towers incorporated into cities' fortifications. It has nothing to do with ziggurat. A tower with "its top in the sky" is ancient Near Eastern cliché for impressive height (see Deut 1:28) and implies neither an attempt to scale the heavens nor an arrogant revolt against divine authority.[38] Ibn Ezra wrote that "the builders of the tower were not fools to believe that they could actually ascend the heavens." Building the city and tower were only means to the perpetuation of a single culture, speaking one language, living in one place. Rather than vanity, making a name is always considered a noble venture, essentially the act of establishing an identity that will endure. "A collective name, as sociologists point out, is one of the

35. Mann, *Book of the Torah*, 37.
36. Hiebert, "Tower of Babel," 56.
37. Anderson, "Unity and Diversity," 76.
38. Hiebert, "Tower of Babel," 37.

primary markers of a common cultural tradition."[39] Some posit that the city itself is the primary symbol of human self-sufficiency, autonomy, and hubris, but the city is merely mentioned with no explicit value judgment on it.

YHWH's parallel and reversing response is not an act of punishment or judgment, but an intervention to introduce cultural difference. That YHWH came down to see the city reflects the ancient Near Eastern view of a two-tiered universe in which the divine and the human inhabit different realms, necessitating divine descent to make contact with the human realm and to act within it; it is no satire of the human pretension of building a tower into heaven. YHWH responds to the builders' cultural uniformity, not to their pride or imperial pretensions. He does not speak about the tower or its height, about the hubris of its builders, about their challenge to divine authority, or about their imperial power. Rather he spoke about humanity's homogeneity: "there is now one people and they all have one language."[40] The versions translate the divine comment from the point of view of the traditional sin and punishment scenario. The NRSV has, "nothing that *they propose to do* will now be impossible for them"; the NAB, "nothing will *later* stop them from doing *whatever they presume* to do." Notice the expansive "whatever they presume to do," and "nothing they propose to do." Both shift the people's planning to the future and make God respond to such possible future. But God's observation is to be rendered in the present perfect tense, "this is what they have begun to do." "All that they plan to do" must refer to the human plans described in the first half of the story, that is, making bricks and building a city and a tower in the hopes of not being dispersed across the earth. That is, based on what they have accomplished already, their plans will succeed, namely, to avoid dispersion by building a city.[41] YHWH then intervenes to introduce the world's cultures, introducing multiple languages and dispersing the people through all the earth. The Yahwist uses *balal* (mix) in alliteration to Babel. With no linguistic meaning as support, exegetes adopted the terms "confuse" and "confound" to imply divine punishment in God's action.[42] God dispersed (verb, *puṣ*) them (not necessarily "scattered them," which often implies enemies or exiles) over the face of all the earth.[43] God's two actions,

---

39. Ibid., 40.
40. Ibid., 41–42.
41. Ibid., 45.
42. Ibid., 47.
43. Ibid., 49.

distinguishing languages and dispersing humanity, explain the origin of the world's cultures and provide an etiology of cultural difference. The narrator represents the drive toward identity and solidarity as the distinctively human impulse and the emergence of difference as the peculiarly divine ambition. The story acknowledges both cultural solidarity and cultural difference and their value.

From Shem to Abram

After the story of the building of city and tower, the narrator picks up the genealogy of Shem from Genesis 10, adding that Shem begot Arpachshad when he was a hundred years old, *two years after the flood*. Genesis 7:6 informs that Noah was six hundred years old when the flood came, 5:32, that he begot Shem, Ham, and Japhet when he was five hundred years old. A hundred years of Shem should be six hundred years of Noah, the year of the flood, not two years before the flood. For a valiant attempt to reconcile this discrepancy, the reader may consult Frederick Cryer.[44] The genealogy fixes on the line of Peleg, sidelining Joktan, and landing at Terah who at seventy years old begot Abram, Nahor, and Haran. With the figure of Abram, the destination of the primeval genealogies is reached. He is the ancestor of the people Israel whose story will occupy the rest of the Hebrew Bible. Israel is not one of the nations in the genealogies. But her origins have been solidly located in Mesopotamia, the cradle of civilization, and her relations with the rest of the world's peoples delineated. She will proceed from the loins of Abram through God's grace and blessing. *Sarai was barren, she had no child* is a brief but important notice. The story will go on to relate that the birth of Israel is a miracle of God. *Terah took his son Abram, his grandson Lot . . . and his daughter-in-law Sarai . . . and brought them out of Ur of the Chaldees, to go to the land of Canaan.* Ur of the Chaldees is anachronistic. It will in the tradition beget stories of Abram in the fire (Hebrew *'ūr*) of the Chaldeans because of his monotheistic faith. The migration of Terah stopped at Haran; the LORD calls Abram to proceed from Haran "to a land that I will show you" (Gen 12:2).

---

44. Cryer, "Interrelationships of Gen 5,32; 10–11."

Tradition

At 11:9, the LXX rendered: "on this account its name was called Confusion, because there the Lord confounded the languages of all the earth." The Greek term used for confusion is *sunchusis*, which can connote fractional strife. In the second century BCE, *Jubilees* 10:18–26 put the "wicked purpose" of building the city and tower in the land of Shinar in the days of Reu, son of Peleg, when people said to themselves, "go to, let us ascend thereby into heaven." They built it for forty-three years. The LORD spoke to the ministering angels who came down with him. He confounded their speech and they no longer understood one another's speech, and ceased building the city and tower. From thence they dispersed into their cities, each according to his language and his nation. "And the Lord sent a mighty wind against the tower and overthrew it upon the earth, and behold it was between Asshur and Babylon in the land of Shinar, and they called its name 'Overthrow'" (*Jub* 10:26). Josephus (ca. 100 CE) interpreted the story of the tower with a Greek political hermeneutic key, using it to polemicize against the Greeks.[45] He harmonized Genesis 10 and 11 by omitting the generations following Japhet, Ham, and Shem. Japhet, Ham, and Shem came down from the mountains and persuaded the others, who were afraid of the flood, to do so (*Ant* 1.109). When they grew in numbers, God commanded them to colonize the earth, "in order that they might not engage in civil strife with one another." They disobeyed fearing that he wanted to disperse them so they can easily be fought. The divine command to colonize the earth is twice given and disobeyed, then the punishment. Rather than a cruel God punishing for no clear reason, Josephus insists on God's *eumeneia* (goodwill, kindness). God almost begged humans to disperse in order not to fight each other and to enjoy the fruits of their lands. The pattern of human contempt for divine providence is central to the *Antiquities*. Likewise, the idea that human disobedience to God leads to human decline and misery, and that material prosperity leads to insolence frequently occurs in Josephus' work.[46] Nimrod was the one who incited humankind to hubris and contempt of God. He established a tyranny and conceived the project of a tower to prevent the consequences of a second flood. In addition, the tower would enable him to take revenge on God for the destruction of his forefathers (*Ant* 1.114). The people followed Nimrod

---

45. Inawlocki, "Josephus' Rewriting of the Babel Narrative," 169.
46. Ibid., 173.

and considered it slavery to submit to God. Noteworthy are the omission of the city, the divine descent, and speech concerning the tower and the builders, also the mention of a common language before the construction of the tower. The mention of Nimrod seeks to harmonize Gen 10:1–32 and Gen 11:1–9. The place was then called Babel because *sunchusis* is the translation of the Hebrew word Babel. In book IV of the *Jewish War*, *sunchusis* is used exclusively to designate political confusion. Josephus focuses on its political dimension: the main divine punishment is, according to Josephus, civil strife, not linguistic diversity. He does not say that the confusion of languages caused a *stasis* (civil strife), as other texts suggest, but that *stasis* was caused by God through the confusion (*Ant* 1.117). Therefore, *stasis* appears as the main divine punishment![47] *Targum Ps-Jonathan* noted that the one language was the language of the sanctuary, (the language) in which the world was created in the beginning. They said to one another: Let us make ourselves an idol at its top, and let us put a sword in its hand, and let it draw up battle formations[48] against (him) before we are scattered. The Memra of the Lord descended with seventy angels corresponding to the seventy nations, each having the language of his people and the characters of its writing in his hand. He scattered them thence upon the face of all the earth into seventy languages, so that one did not know what the other said, and they killed one another. The notation in 11:28 that *Haran died before Terah, his father, in his native land, in Ur of the Chaldees*, was brought forward into the story of the tower. Ur of the Chaldees is literally "fire of the Chaldeans." *Targum Ps-Jonathan* relates that Nimrod when he cast Abram into the furnace of fire because he would not worship his idol, the fire had no power to burn him. Then Haran was undecided, and he said: "If Nimrod triumphs, I will be on his side; but if Abram triumphs, I will be on his side." And when all the people who were there saw that the fire had no power over Abram, they said to themselves: "Is not Haran the brother of Abram full of divination and sorcery? It is he who uttered charms over the fire so that it would not burn his brother. Immediately fire fell from the heavens on high and consumed him; and Haran died in the sight of Terah his father, being burned in the land of his birth in the furnace of fire which

---

47. Ibid., 180.

48. *GenR* 38:6 reports in the name of Rabbi Leazar (Eleazar ben Pedat, first half of fourth century CE) the tradition that the tower was topped by an idol with a sword in its hand to wage war against God.

the Chaldeans had made for Abram his brother."[49] Abram appears thus as the first monotheist.

The Christian tradition very early interpreted the story of the tower in terms of sin and punishment. Augustine found the city of man appearing in the generation of the tower: "But from the time they built a tower to heaven, a symbol of godless exaltation, the city or society of the wicked became apparent."[50] Jerome wrote: "Indeed, when the tower was being built up against God, those who were building it were disbanded for their own welfare. The conspiracy was evil. The dispersion was of true benefit even to those who were dispersed."[51] Some Jewish tradition filtered into Christian exegesis. Ephrem inserted the tradition about Nimrod: "In addition, because of their new languages . . . war broke out among them . . . It was Nimrod who scattered them. It was also he who seized Babel and became its first ruler. If Nimrod had not scattered them each to his own place, he would not have been able to take that place where they all lived before."[52] That goes even for the tradition of Abram professing God in the fire: "In place of what we read [in the LXX] as 'in the territory of the Chaldeans,' in Hebrew it has in 'ur Chesdim,' that is, 'in the fire of the Chaldeans.' Moreover the Hebrews . . . hand on a story of this sort to the effect that Abraham was put into the fire because he refused to worship the fire, which the Chaldeans honor and that he escaped through God's help and fled from the fire of idolatry . . . 'Aran died before the face of Thera in the land of his birth *in the fire of the Chaldeans,*' that is, because he refused to worship fire, he was consumed by fire."[53]

---

49. A similar tradition appears in *GenR* 38:13 in the name of Rabbi Hiyya (Hiyya the Great, about 180–230 CE).

50. Augustine, *City of God*, 16.10, in ACCS, 172.

51. Jerome, *Homilies* 21, in ACCS, 169.

52. Ephrem, *Commentary on Genesis*, 8.3.2–8.4.2, in ACCS, 169.

53. Jerome, *Hebrew Questions on Genesis*, 11.28, in ACCS, 172–73.

Conclusion

The primeval story has been one of divine grace and forbearance. The man and woman no sooner enter the garden than they transgress against YHWH God, just as Israel would no sooner receive the covenant of love at Sinai than they would fall into the sin of idolatry (Exod 32)! God shows the same self-limitation in walking with humanity as he would with Israel. He blesses and curses, rewards and punishes, yet by no means leaves humanity to its own deserts, rather takes up the relationship and holds himself always readily available. Despite the heart of humankind remaining evil from youth, after the flood as before, "God decides to go with a wicked world, come what may. In committing to an imperfect world, God determines to take suffering into his own self and bear it for the sake of the future of the world."[1]

Along the way, we learned of the beneficence and generosity of a God who took joy in preparing a pleasant environment for his creatures, yet obedience to whose word is life and disobedience death. We learned of the dynamics of temptation, of trust and infidelity, of sin and guilt as forces within and outside humans, of Lamech's megalomania, of the heart of humans scheming only evil from youth, and the generation of the tower's quest for a name. We witnessed the building of cities and flourishing of culture, but also fratricide, drunkenness and its effects, and a father cursing his son to slavery. Through all this, the Garden stands as symbol of God's intentions for humankind and creation, the flood of the ruin that humans can bring to their world. Yet, the rainbow stands as perpetual sign that God will never disengage from his world, come what may: "all the days of the earth, seedtime and harvest, cold and heat, summer and winter, and day and night, shall not cease" (Gen 8:22).

Muilenburg helps us pull the threads together. He traces four paradigmatic episodes in the primeval history: the Paradise Story (Gen 2:4b—3:24),

1. Fretheim, "God of the Flood Story," 33.

the Two Brothers (Gen 4:1–16), the Cohabitation of Divine Beings with Human Women (Gen 6:1–4), and the Tower of Babel (Gen 11:1–9). In each case, the same theological movement is at play—the sin of humans is followed by divine judgment/punishment and divine grace beyond the judgment.[2] The disobedience of the first couple is punished by expulsion from the garden, but YHWH not only relents from the decree of death but also made clothes for the ashamed couple. Cain's fratricide is followed by expulsion from fertile land, yet YHWH puts a sign of divine protection on him. The mixing of divine beings and human women calls down the flood, but not only is Noah spared but also Yahweh commits himself never again to curse the earth despite the inveterate evil of the human heart. The fourth episode seems at first to lack the element of divine grace: the hubris of the tower builders is punished with dispersion and the story seems to end there; however, on closer examination it seen that

> the merciful grace of YHWH which persists through all the narratives of the prologue save the last now overcomes the final treason of the nations in their zealous efforts to build civilization without God . . . Abram becomes the embodiment of divine grace.[3]

We end this commentary with the dictum of Irenaeus.

> For the glory of God is a living man; and the life of man consists in beholding God. For if the manifestation of God which is made by means of the creation, affords life to all living in the earth, much more does that revelation of the Father which comes through the Word, give life to those who see God.[4]

---

2. Muilenburg, "Abraham and the Nations," 389.

3. Ibid., 393. I have here reused what I wrote in Okoye, *Israel and the Nations*, 44.

4. *Against Heresies*, 4.34.5–7.

Bibliography

Adams, Edwards. "Retrieving the Earth from the Conflagration: 2 Peter 3:5–13 and the Environment." In *Ecological Hermeneutics*, edited by David Horrel et al., 108–20. London: T. & T. Clark, 2010.

Alter, Robert. *The Art of Biblical Narrative*. New York: Basic, 1981.

———. *Genesis: Translation and Commentary*. New York: Norton, 1996.

Alter, Robert, and Frank Kermode, eds. *The Literary Guide to the Bible*. Cambridge: Harvard University Press, 1987.

Amit, Yairah. *The Book of Judges: The Art of Editing*. Leiden: Brill, 1999.

———. *Hidden Polemics in Biblical Narrative*. Leiden: Brill, 2000.

———. *Reading Biblical Narratives. Literary Criticism and the Hebrew Bible*. Minneapolis: Fortress, 2001.

Anderson, Bernhard W. "Unity and Diversity in God's Creation: A Study of the Babel Story." *Currents in Theology and Mission* 5 (1978) 69–81.

Augustine of Hippo. *Teaching Christianity (De Doctrina Christiana)*. Translated with notes by Edmund Hill. New York: New City, 1996.

Bal, Mieke. *Lethal Love: Feminist Literary Readings of Biblical Love Stories*. Bloomington: Indiana University Press, 1987.

Bar-Efrat, Shimeon. *Narrative Art in the Bible*. Sheffield: Almond, 1989.

Barr, James. *The Garden of Eden and the Hope of Immortality*. Minneapolis: Fortress, 1993.

Benedict XVI. *Verbum Domini*. Post-synodal apostolic exhortation. Editrice Vaticana, 2010.

Berlin, Adele. *Poetics and Interpretation of Biblical Narrative*. Winona Lake, IN: Eisenbrauns, 1994.

Bird, Phyllis. "Genesis I–III as a Source for Contemporary Theology of Sexuality." *Ex Auditu* 3 (1987) 31–44.

Blenkinsopp, Joseph. *Creation, Un-Creation, Re-Creation. A Discursive Commentary on Genesis 1–11*. London: T. & T. Clark, 2011.

———. "The Midianite-Kenite Hypothesis Revisited and the Origins of Judah." *JSOT* 33 (2008) 131–53.

Bonino, José Miguez. "Covenant of Life: A Meditation on Genesis 9:1–17." *Ecumenical Review* 33 (2010) 341–45.

Bradley, L. Richard. "The Curse of Canaan and the American Negro." *Concordia Theological Monthly* 42 (1971) 100–110.

Brueggemann, Walter. *Genesis*. Interpretation. A Bible Commentary for Teaching and Preaching. Atlanta: John Knox, 1982.

———. *Theology of the Old Testament: Testimony, Dispute, Advocacy.* Minneapolis: Fortress, 1997.

Cassuto, Umberto. *A Commentary on the Book of Genesis.* Pt. 1, *From Adam to Noah.* Jerusalem: Magnes, 1961.

———. *A Commentary on the Book of Genesis.* Pt. 2, *From Noah to Abraham.* Jerusalem: Magnes, 1964.

Catechism of the Catholic Church. New York: Doubleday, 1994, 1998.

Charlesworth, James H. *The Good and Evil Serpent: How a Universal Symbol Became Christianized.* New Haven: Yale University Press, 2010.

———. *Old Testament Pseudepigrapha.* Vol. 2. New York: Doubleday, 1985.

Clines, David. "The Significance of the 'Sons of God' Episode (Genesis 6:1–4) in the Context of the Primeval History (Genesis 1–11)." *JSOT* 13 (1979) 33–46.

Compendium of the Social Doctrine of the Church. Vatican: Libreria Editrice Vaticana, 2004.

Copher, Charles B. "Three Thousand Years of Biblical Interpretation with Reference to Black Peoples." In Wilmore, *African American Religious Studies,* 105–28.

Cotter, David. *Genesis.* Berit Olam. Collegeville: Liturgical, 2003.

Croatto, J. Severino. "A Reading of the Story of the Tower of Babel from the Perspective of Non-Identity: Gen 11:1–9 in the Context of Its Production." In *Teaching the Bible: The Discourses and Politics of Biblical Pedagogy,* edited by Fernando Segovia and Mary Ann Tolbert, 203–23. Maryknoll: Orbis, 1998.

Cryer, Frederick. "The Interrelationships of Gen 5:32; 11,10–11 and the Chronology of the Flood (Gen 6–9)." *Bib* 66 (1985) 241–61.

Danby, Herbert. *The Mishnah.* Translated from the Hebrew with introduction and notes. Oxford: Clarendon, 1933.

The Documents of Vatican II. Edited by Walter Abbot. London: Chapman, 1966.

Dozeman, Thomas, et al., eds. *The Pentateuch: International Perspectives on Current Research.* Tübingen: Mohr Siebeck, 2011.

Dunn, James D. G. *The Theology of Paul the Apostle.* Grand Rapids: Eerdmans, 2006.

Elowsky, Joel C., ed. *We Believe in the Holy Spirit.* Downers Grove: IVP Academic, 2009.

Felder, Cain Hope. "Race, Racism and the Biblical Narratives." In *Stony the Road We Trod,* 127–45.

———. *Stony the Road We Trod: African American Biblical Interpretation.* Minneapolis: Fortress, 1991.

Fergusson, David. "Interpreting the Story of Creation: A Case Study in the Dialogue between Theology and Science." In *Genesis and Christian Theology,* edited by Nathan McDonald et al., 155–74. Grand Rapids: Eerdmans, 2012.

Fewell, Danna Nolan, and David Gunn. "Shifting the Blame." In *Gender, Power, and Promise: The Subject of the Bible's First Story,* 22–38. Nashville: Abingdon, 1993.

Fleming, Fraser. *The Truth about Science and Religion: From the Big Bang to Neuroscience.* Eugene, OR: Wipf & Stock, 2016.

Florence, Anna Carter. "After the Flood Genesis 9:18–28." *Journal for Preachers* (Advent 2001) 41–45.

Fokkelman, Jan P. *Narrative Art and Poetry in the Books of Samuel.* 3 parts. Assen, Amsterdam: Van Gorcum, 1981–1993.

———. *Narrative Art in Genesis.* Assen, Amsterdam: Van Gorcum, 1975.

———. *Reading Biblical Narrative: An Introductory Guide.* Louisville: Westminster John Knox, 1999.

Fouts, David M. "Peleg in Gen 10:25." *JETS* 41/1 (1998) 17–21.

Fox, Everett. *The Five Books of Moses*. New York: Schocken, 1995.

Freedman, H., and Maurice Simon, eds. *Midrash Rabbah: Genesis*. London: Soncino, 1977.

Fretheim, Terence. "God of the Flood Story and Natural Disasters." *Calvin Theological Journal* 43 (2008) 21–34.

———. *The Suffering of God: An Old Testament Perspective*. Philadelphia: Fortress, 1984.

Garsiel, Moshe. *The First Book of Samuel: A Literary Study of Comparative Structures, Analogies and Parallels*. Ramat Gan, Israel: Revivim, 1985.

Goldingay, John. *Israel's Gospel*. Vol. 1 of *Old Testament Theology*. Downers Grove: IVP Academic, 2003.

Goppelt, Leonhard. *Typos: The Typological Interpretation of the Old Testament in the New*. 1939. Wipf & Stock, 2002.

The Green Bible. Understanding the Bible's Powerful Message for the Earth. Harper Collins, 2008.

Gunn, David. *The Fate of Saul: An Interpretation of a Biblical Story*. JSOTSup 14. Sheffield: JSOT Press, 1980.

———. "New Directions in the Study of Biblical Hebrew Narrative." *JSOT* 39 (1987) 65–75.

Gunn, David and Danna Fewell. *Narrative in the Hebrew Bible*. New York: Oxford University Press, 1993.

———. "Varieties of Interpretation: Genesis 4 through 2000 Years." In Gunn and Fewell, *Narrative in the Hebrew Bible*, 12–33.

Habel, Norman C., ed. *The Birth, the Curse and the Greening of Earth: An Ecological Reading of Genesis 1–11*. Sheffield: Phoenix, 2011.

———. *Readings from the Perspective of Earth*. Earth Bible 1. Sheffield: Sheffield Academic, 2000.

Habel, Norman, and Peter Trudinger, eds. *Exploring Ecological Hermeneutics*. Atlanta: SBL, 2008.

Hamilton, Victor P. *The Book of Genesis, Chapters 1–17*. Grand Rapids: Eerdmans, 1990.

Hayes, Zachary. *The Gift of Being: A Theology of Creation*. Collegeville: Liturgical, 2001.

Heidel, Alexander. *The Gilgamesh Epic and Old Testament Parallels*. 2nd ed. Chicago: University of Chicago Press, 1949.

Heschel, Abraham Joshua. *The Sabbath: Its Meaning for Modern Man*. New York: Noonday, 1975.

Hiebert, Theodore. "Tower of Babel and the Origin of the World's Cultures." *JBL* 126/1 (2007) 29–58.

Horrel, David, et al., eds. *Ecological Hermeneutics*. London: T. & T. Clark, 2010.

House, Paul. "God's Design and Postmodernism: Recent Approaches to Old Testament Theology." In *The Old Testament in the Life of God's People: Essays in Honor of Elmer A. Martens*, edited by Jon Isaak, 29–54. Winona Lake: Eisenbrauns, 2009.

Humphreys, W. Lee. *The Character of God in the Book of Genesis*. Louisville: Westminster John Knox, 2001.

Inawlocki, Sabrina. "Josephus' Rewriting of the Babel Narrative (Gen 11:1–9)." *Journal for the Study of Judaism* 37/2 (2006) 169–91.

Irenaeus. *Against Heresies*. In *The Faith of the Early Fathers*, edited by William A. Jurgens, 1:84–107. Collegeville: Liturgical, 1970.

———. *Against Heresies*. In *Ante-Nicene Fathers*, vol. 1, edited by Alexander Roberts et al., translated by Alexander Roberts and William Rambaut. Buffalo, NY: Christian

Literature, 1885. Revised and edited for New Advent by Kevin Knight. http://www.newadvent.org/fathers/0103.htm.

———. *Proof of the Apostolic Preaching*. Translated and annotated by Joseph P. Smith. London: Longmans, Green, 1952.

Jeremias, Joachim. "Paradeisos." In *TDNT*, 5:765–73.

Jewish Study Bible. Edited by Adele Berlin and Marc Zvi Brettler. Jewish Publication Society. Oxford: Oxford University Press, 1999.

Jobling, David. "Myth and Its Limits in Genesis 2.4b—3.24." In *The Sense of Biblical Narrative: Structural Analyses in the Hebrew Bible*, 2:17–43. JSOTSup 7. Sheffield: JSOT Press, 1986.

Josephus. "Antiquities of the Jews." In *The Works of Josephus*, 27–542. Complete and unabridged. New updated ed. Translated by William Whiston. Peabody: Hendrickson, 1987.

Justin Martyr. *Saint Justin Martyr*. Translated by Thomas B. Falls. Fathers of the Church 6. Washington: Catholic University of America Press, 1948.

Kaminsky, Joel. "Reclaiming a Theology of Election: Favoritism and the Joseph Story." *Perspectives in Religious Studies* 31/2 (2004) 135–52.

Kelly, Declan. "Discuss and Evaluate the Strengths and Weaknesses of Narrative Criticism as a Tool for a Theological Reading of the Old Testament." http://www.academia.edu/10033083/Narrative_Criticism_and_a_Theological_Reading_of_the_Old_Testament.

Kling, David W. *The Bible in History: How the Texts Have Shaped the Times*. Oxford: Oxford University Press, 2004.

Kreider, Glenn R. "Flood as Bad as It Gets: Never Again Will God Destroy the Earth." *Bibliotheca Sacra* 171 (2014) 418–39.

Kugel, James L. *The Bible as It Was*. Cambridge: Harvard University Press, 1997.

Kugel, James L., and Rowan A. Greer. *Early Biblical Interpretation*. Philadelphia: Westminster, 1986.

Lanser, Susan. "Feminist Criticism in the Garden: Inferring Genesis 2–3." *Semeia* 41–44 (1988) 67–84.

Levenson, Jon Douglas. *Creation and the Persistence of Evil: The Jewish Drama of Divine Omnipotence*. Princeton: Princeton University Press, 1988.

———. *The Death and Resurrection of the Beloved Son*. New Haven: Yale University Press, 1993.

———. "The Universal Horizon of Biblical Particularism." In *Ethnicity and the Bible*, edited by Mark G. Brett, 146–69. Leiden: Brill, 1996.

———. "Why Jews Are Not Interested in Biblical Theology." *Judaic Perspectives on Ancient Israel*, edited by Jacob Neusner et al., 281–307. Philadelphia: Fortress, 1987.

Lewis, Jack P. "The Offering of Abel (Gen 4:4): A History of Interpretation." *JETS* 37/4 (1994) 481–96.

Louth, Andrew, ed. *Genesis 1–11*. Ancient Christian Commentary on Scripture, Old Testament, 1. Downers Grove: InterVarsity, 2001.

MacCulloch, John Arnott. "Serpent Worship." In *Encyclopedia of Religion and Ethics*, edited by James Hastings, 11:403. London: T. & T. Clark, 2003.

Malina, Bruce J., and John J. Pilch. *Biblical Social Values and Their Meaning: A Handbook*. Peabody: Hendrickson, 1993.

Mann, Thomas. *The Book of the Torah: The Narrative Integrity of the Pentateuch*. Atlanta: John Knox, 1988. 2nd ed. Eugene, OR: Cascade, 2013.

Matthews, Victor H., and Don C. Benjamin. *Old Testament Parallels*. Rev. ed. New York: Paulist, 1991.

Mbiti, John. *Introduction to African Religion*. New York: Praeger, 1975.

McDonald, Nathan, et al., eds. *Genesis and Christian Theology*. Grand Rapids: Eerdmans, 2012.

Meyers, Carol. *Discovering Eve: Ancient Israelite Women in Context*. Oxford: Oxford University Press, 1998.

Milgrom, Jacob. "Repentance." In *IDB*, 5:736–38.

Miller, Patrick D. *Genesis 1–11: Studies in Structure and Theme*. JSOTSup 8. Sheffield: JSOT Press, 1978.

The Mishnah. Translated from the Hebrew with introduction and notes by Herbert Danby. Oxford: Clarendon, 1933.

Moberly, R. W. L. *The Old Testament of the Old Testament*. Minneapolis: Fortress, 1992.

———. *Old Testament Theology: Reading the Hebrew Bible as Christian Scripture*. Grand Rapids: Baker Academic, 2013.

———. *Theology of the Book of Genesis*. 1st ed. Cambridge: Cambridge University Press, 2009.

Muilenburg, James. "Abraham and the Nations: Blessing and World History." *Int* 19 (1965) 387–98.

New African Bible. Nairobi: Paulines, 2011.

Neusner, Jacob, et al., eds. *Judaic Perspectives on Ancient Israel*. Philadelphia: Fortress, 1987.

Nickelsburg, George W. E., and James C. VanderKam. *I Enoch: A New Translation*. Minneapolis: Fortress, 2004.

Noth, Martin. *Old Testament World*. Philadelphia: Fortress, 1966.

Okoye, James Chukwuma. "An Examination of the Non-Literal Exegesis in Genesis 1–11 in the Pseudo-Jonathan Targum." PhD diss., Oxford University, 1980.

———. *Scripture in the Church: The Synod on the Word of God and the Post-Synodal Exhortation Verbum Domini*. Collegeville: Liturgical, 2011.

———. *Israel and the Nations: A Mission Theology of the Old Testament*. Maryknoll: Orbis, 2006.

Old Testament in the Life of God's People: Essays in Honor of Elmer A. Martens. Edited by Jon Isaak. Winona Lake, IN: Eisenbrauns, 2009.

Ollenburger, Ben C., ed. *Old Testament Theology: Flowering and Future*. Rev. ed. Sources for Biblical and Theological Study 1. Winona Lake: Eisenbrauns, 2004.

Origen. *Contra Celsum (Against Celsus)*. Translated with introduction and notes by Henry Chadwick. Cambridge: Cambridge University Press, 1953.

———. *De Principiis (The Fundamental Doctrines)*. In *The Faith of the Early Fathers*, edited by William A. Jurgens, 1:190–200. Collegeville: Liturgical, 1970.

Otzen, B. "Yeṣer." In *TDOT*, 6:265.

Pedersen, Johs. *Israel: Its Life and Culture*. Vols. 1–2. London: Oxford University Press, 1926.

Penchansky, David. *What Rough Beast? Images of God in the Hebrew Bible*. Louisville: Westminster John Knox, 1999.

Pentateuch with Targum Onkelos, Haphtaroth and Rashi's Commentary: Genesis. Translated and annotated by M. Rosenbaum and A. M. Silbermann. New York: Hebrew Publishing, 1935.

Petersen, David. "Genesis 6:1–4: Yahweh and the Organization of the Cosmos." *JSOT* 13 (1979) 47–64.

Pilch, John J., and Bruce J. Malina. *Biblical Social Values and Their Meaning: A Handbook.* Peabody: Hendrickson, 1993.

Plaut, W. Gunther, ed. *The Torah: A Modern Commentary.* Rev. ed. New York: Union for Reform Judaism Press, 2006.

Pontifical Biblical Commission. *The Interpretation of the Bible in the Church.* Vatican City: Libreria Editrice Vaticana, 1993.

———. *The Jewish People and Their Sacred Scriptures in the Christian Bible.* Vatican City, 2002.

———. *The Inspiration and Truth of Sacred Scripture.* Collegeville: Liturgical, 2014.

Pope Francis. *Laudato Si'.* Encyclical letter on care for our common world. Vatican City, 2016.

Pope John Paul II. Letter to Rev. George V. Coyne. Director of the Vatican Observatory, June 1, 1988.

Pope Pius XII. *Humani generis.* Encyclical letter on the inspiration of the scriptures. 1950.

Porter Stanley E. "The Pauline Concept of Original Sin, in Light of Rabbinic Background." *Tyndale Bulletin* 41/1 (1990) 3–20.

Pritchard, James B., ed. *Ancient Near Eastern Texts Relating to the Old Testament.* 3rd ed. Princeton: Princeton University Press, 1969.

Rad, Gerhard von. *Commentary on Genesis.* Rev. ed. Phildelphia: Westminster, 1972.

Ratzinger, Joseph. *"In the Beginning . . .": A Catholic Understanding of the Story of Creation and Fall.* Grand Rapids: Eerdmans, 1986.

Ricoeur, Paul. *The Symbolism of Evil.* Boston: Beacon, 1967.

Ross, Allen, P. "The Dispersion of the Nations in Genesis 11:1–9." *Bibliotheca Sacra* 138 (1981) 119–38.

———. "The Table of Nations in Genesis 10—Its Content." *Bibliotheca Sacra* 138 (1980) 22–34.

———. "The Table of Nations in Genesis 10: Structure." *Bibliotheca Sacra* 137 (1980) 340–53.

Rowley, H. H. *From Joseph to Joshua: Biblical Traditions in the Light of Archaeology.* Oxford: Oxford University Press, 1950.

———. "Moses and Monotheism." In Rowley, *From Joseph to Joshua,* 35–63.

Sailhamer, John H. *The Pentateuch as Narrative: A Biblical-Theological Commentary.* Grand Rapids: Zondervan, 1992.

Sarna, Nahum M. *Understanding Genesis: The World of the Bible in the Light of History.* New York: Schoken, 1966.

Sasson, Jack M. "The 'Tower of Babel' as Clue to the Redactional Structuring of the Primeval History [Gen. 1—11:9]." In *The Bible World: Essays in Honor of Cyrus H. Gordon,* edited by Gary Rendsburg et al., 211–19. New York: KTAV, 1980.

Segovia, Fernando, and Mary Ann Tolbert, eds. *Teaching the Bible: The Discourses and Politics of Biblical Pedagogy.* Maryknoll: Orbis, 1998.

Sheridan, Mark, ed. *Genesis 12–50.* Ancient Christian Commentary on Scripture. Downers Grove: InterVarsity, 2001.

Simonetti, Manlio. *Biblical Interpretation in the Early Church: An Historical Introduction to Patristic Exegesis.* Edinburgh: T. & T. Clark, 1994.

Skinner, John. *A Critical and Exegetical Commentary on Genesis.* New York: Scribner, 1910.

Smith, David. "What Hope after Babel? Diversity and Community in Gen 11:1–9; Exod 1:1–14; Zeph 3:1–13 and Acts 2:1–3." *Horizons in Biblical Theology* 18/1 (1996) 169–91.

Smith, Mark S. *The Priestly Vision of Genesis 1.* Minneapolis: Fortress, 2010.

Speiser, E. A. *Genesis.* New York: Doubleday, 1964.

Spero, Shubert. "Why Was God Optimistic after the Flood?" *Jewish Bible Quarterly* 30/4 (2002) 235–41.

Sternberg, Meir. *The Poetics of Biblical Narrative: Ideological Literature and the Drama of Reading.* Bloomington: Indiana University Press, 1985.

Sugirtharajah, R. S., ed. *Voices from the Margin: Interpreting the Bible in the Third World.* Rev. ed. Maryknoll: Orbis, 1995.

Targum Neofiti 1: Genesis. Translated with introduction and notes by Martin McNamara. Aramaic Bible 1A. Collegeville: Liturgical, 1992.

The Targum Onqelos to Genesis. Translated with introduction and notes by Bernard Grossfeld. Aramaic Bible 6. Collegeville: Liturgical, 1988.

Targum Pseudo-Jonathan: Genesis. Translated with introduction and notes by Michael Maher. Aramaic Bible 1B. Collegeville: Liturgical, 1992.

Trible, Phyllis. *God and the Rhetoric of Sexuality.* Philadelphi: Fortress, 1978.

Urbach, Ephraim E. *The Sages: Their Concepts and Beliefs.* Vol. 1. Jerusalem: Magnes, 1975.

VanMaaren, John. "The Adam-Christ Typology in Paul and its Development in the Early Church Fathers." *Tyndale Bulletin* 64.2 (2013) 275–297.

Vermes, Geza. "The Targumic Versions of Genesis 4:3–16." In *Post-Biblical Jewish Studies,* 92–126. Leiden: Brill, 1975.

Walsh, Jerome T. "Gen 2:4b—3:24: A Synchronic Approach." *JBL* 96 (1977) 161–77.

Warrior, Robert Allen. "A Native American Perspective: Canaanites, Cowboys, and Indians." In Sugirtharajah, *Voices from the Margin,* 277–85.

Weinfeld, Moshe. "God the Creator in Genesis 1 and in the Prophecy of Second Isaiah." *Tarbiz* [Hebrew] 37 (1968) 122–26.

Weingreen, J. *From Bible to Mishnah: The Continuity of Tradition.* Manchester: Manchester University Press, 1976.

Wenham, Gordon J. *Story as Torah: Reading Old Testament Narrative Ethically.* Grand Rapids: Baker Academic, 2004.

Westermann, Claus. *Genesis 1–11.* Minneapolis: Fortress, 1994.

Whedbee, J. William. *The Bible and the Comic Vision.* Philadelphia: Fortress, 2009.

Wilmore, G. S., ed. *African American Religious Studies: An Interdisciplinary Anthology.* Durham: Duke University Press, 1989.

Wittenberg, Gunther. "'. . . Let Canaan Be His Slave' (Gen 9: 26): Is Ham also Cursed?" *Journal of Theology for Southern Africa* 74 (1991) 46–56.

Zenger, Erich and Karl Lönig. *To Begin With, God Created . . . : Biblical Theologies of Creation.* Collegeville: Liturgical, 2000.

Zobel, Hans-Jürgen. "*Kena'an.*" In *TDOT,* 7:211–28.

Index of Ancient Sources

❖

PSEUDEPIGRAPHA

❖

DEAD SEA SCROLLS

❖

JOSEPHUS

❧

ROMAN CATHOLIC WORKS

Catechism of the Catholic Church

9 781532 609916